garden people

THE PHOTOGRAPHS OF VALERIE FINNIS

Ursula Buchan

with Anna Pavord
and Brent Elliott

with 229 color illustrations

 Thames & Hudson

This book is dedicated to the memory of Valerie Finnis
(31 October 1924 to 17 October 2006) – mentor and friend.

First published in 2007 in hardcover in the United States of
America by Thames & Hudson Inc., 500 Fifth Avenue, New York,
New York 10110

thamesandhudsonusa.com

Library of Congress Catalog Card Number 2006908245

ISBN-13: 978-0-500-51353-8
ISBN-10: 0-500-51353-8

Printed and bound in China by Imago

Front endpapers Papaver rhoeas 'Fairy Wings'.
Back endpapers Papaver nudicaule 'Constance
Finnis'.
Half-title One of Valerie's exuberant arrangements
of flowers and fruit gathered from The Dower House
garden in August, including lilies, roses, *Kniphofia*,
asters, gentians and Colchicum.
Title-page Valerie Finnis gardening, at the family
home in Reigate, most unusually in a dress. *Below,
left to right Anthemis tinctoria*; Valerie and David
weeding in The Dower House garden, with Kate
the pug; a leaf of *Macleaya cordata*, the Plume
Poppy; Constance Finnis, hoeing the vegetables in
her garden in Reigate, with Posy the pug; *Petasites
japonicus* var. *giganteus*; Sir David Scott, aged 90,
scything in the garden at The Dower House.

CONTENTS

introduction A LIFELONG FASCINATION

When Valerie Finnis acquired her first proper camera in 1955, she began a lifelong fascination with capturing on film both the plants she loved and her wide and eclectic circle of horticulturally inclined contemporaries and friends. Over the course of almost four decades, until the 1990s, she assembled a truly astonishing archive of pictures, mainly on 2¼-inch square transparencies – some 50,000 in total. The vast majority were taken with a Rolleiflex camera, given to her by Wilhelm Schacht, a good friend, who was himself an accomplished flower photographer and the Curator of the Munich Botanical Garden.

The photographs have a remarkable quality, the result of Valerie's almost preternatural powers of observation, coupled with an ebullient personality and an ability to connect with her subjects, and they provide an evocative record of a world which now seems strangely distant from our own. Despite the growth in professional garden photography and advances in both techniques and technology, Valerie is still acknowledged by modern practitioners of the art as one of the finest plant photographers that there has ever been, and a strong influence on those who came after her. She was notable for a 'natural' style, particularly evident in her collections of flowers, gathered from her garden in every season of the year. Her formidable talents as a gardener, her encyclopaedic knowledge of plants, and her 'eye' combined to produce a highly individual body of work, with great charm and immediate appeal.

Valerie Finnis was born in Crowborough in Sussex on 31 October 1924, the second of two daughters of Commander

Previous page (*above*) Sir David Scott at The Dower House, aged 90, with Old Roses from his garden – behind him is a magnificent *Carpenteria californica* planted in 1911; (*below, left to right*) April flowers, including dwarf narcissi and *Anemone pavonina*; July flowers with *Phlox* 'Chatahoochee', garden pinks and *Clematis* 'Bill Mackenzie'; an arrangement picked on Christmas Eve, with *Correa*, *Petasites* and *Prunus subhirtella* 'Autumnalis'.

Above Valerie's mother, Constance, and her pug, Posy, in her garden at Martinhoe, Reigate.
Opposite Valerie named many plants after friends and family: on the left is a strain of Iceland poppy, *Papaver nudicaule* 'Constance Finnis' and on the right, a garden pink, *Dianthus* 'Constance Finnis'.

Steriker and Constance Finnis. Her mother was a talented and keen gardener whose name lives on in a strain of Iceland poppies, *Papaver nudicaule* 'Constance Finnis', as well as a dianthus (garden pink); her father was a naval officer who retired early from the service. By the age of five, the family was settled in Earlswood, near Reigate in Surrey, and the young Valerie had already shown a precocious interest in gardening, encouraged by her mother, who gave her a little garden to cultivate. From her grandmother she received the double daisy 'Rob Roy' and the advice to 'treat these plants reverently – they're people'.

At boarding school at Hayes Court in Kent, which she attended from the age of 13, Valerie was given a plot to look after. Homesick, she found consolation in gardening, thanks to a friendly head gardener and an enlightened headmistress who recognized her horticultural talents. By her own confession she was not very academic, but was good at sport and, more particularly, drama – perhaps inspired by her teacher, a young actor called Alec Guinness.

The outbreak of war in September 1939 brought this happy
situation to an abrupt end. Her father was recalled to the service,
which entailed a move to Gosforth, near Newcastle, and life
in a block of flats. But Constance made a garden in neglected
allotments nearby, helped by Valerie in her holidays. Hayes
Court was thought too close to London for safety and was
closed; Valerie had to move to Downe House School, near
Newbury. Although she was 'shattered' to leave her Hayes Court
garden, it was to prove most fortuitous for her future career.

At Downe House Valerie made friends with a young gardener,
Mary Young, who allowed her to help her when she should have
been playing cricket. Mary had been trained at the Waterperry
Horticultural School for Women. The Principal there was the
extraordinary Miss Beatrix Havergal, who as a young gardener
had laid out the tennis courts at Downe House.

By the time Valerie left school in 1942, Waterperry had been
established ten years and, when the subject of Valerie's future

Valerie Finnis spent many years of her life at
Waterperry, both as student and teacher: in these
three photographs she is seen in her potting shed
and among rock plants in the summer uniform
of white, short-sleeved shirt and green dungarees.

An uncharacteristically stagey arrangement of early
summer flowers (*above*); *opposite* are an early summer
composition and an early spring posy. Many of
Valerie's best-selling images for cards and calendars
were her arrangements of flowers, all picked from her
own garden. *Page 15* A collection of jewel-like alpines
in 3-inch clay pots, including drabas, dionysias,
campanulas and saxifrages. These were the rock plants
which Valerie loved the best, and that she grew
superlatively well.

career came up, horticulture won over both the women's services
and the stage – fortunately for British gardening. She worked
first as a trainee gardener, then member of staff for 28 years until
1970, running the Alpine Department, and for many years lived
in a flat at the top of Shotover House, near Wheatley, home
of Colonel John Miller, who was the Queen's Crown Equerry.

In a book written about Waterperry, Valerie's qualities are
affectionately recalled: 'Many former students will admit that,
given a choice of departments, they would plump for working
in the little Alpine Nursery tucked behind the house … where
Valerie Finnis was in charge. Perhaps it was a soft option
physically … but Valerie Finnis herself ensured that it was
an exciting department to be in. Volatile and amusing with a
strong histrionic streak, and blessed with a remarkable memory
and feeling for plants, she charmed the students as indeed she
charmed Miss H.[avergal] in whose eyes she could do no
wrong. She was not interested in working for the National

Diploma; instead she took lessons on photography from [the] taxi-man Walde …'

At Waterperry, after the war, she built up an extensive collection of alpine plants, eventually propagating an amazing 50,000 plants a year, of which 7,000 were saxifrages, many of them the early-flowering and demanding Kabschia and Engleria types. In 1947, she exhibited alpines for the first time at the Chelsea Flower Show, at one end of the stand where the famous Waterperry 'Royal Sovereign' strawberries were staged. This was the start of many exhibits at Chelsea and other shows.

From 1955, with her first expensive camera, plant photography became a major interest and Valerie's talents were soon recognized: Dr Warburg, one of the authors of the standard work, *Flora of the British Isles*, commissioned photographs for an article he was writing on crocuses. By this time her father was ill, and she was making frequent journeys to Reigate to visit him. She needed extra money, so sent two rolls of film to the greetings card company, Gordon Fraser; they were all accepted. The music company E.M.I. bought 12 transparencies for record sleeves, and J. Walter Thompson used her pictures of vegetables in advertisements for fertilizer. She was launched as a photographer, even though, as she said, 'I never took more than one exposure because it was too expensive'. In 1961 she displayed photographs at Kodak's head office and also won a Gold Medal for them from the RHS. Her pictures appeared in books, for example Anna Griffith's *Collins Guide to Alpines and Rock Garden Plants* (see page 126), first published in 1964, and colour magazines, such as *The Field*. Groups of plants for calendars were very popular, too.

She had also acquired an enviable reputation as lecturer, judge and alpine plant expert, and Miss Havergal was tolerant of the time that this took: in 1961, she was invited as guest botanist on a

David and Valerie on their wedding day in 1970.
An hour after they were married at Weekley church
in Northamptonshire, they were out in the garden
weeding.

Opposite left The garden seen from an upstairs room,
and reached from The Dower House by crossing
a courtyard and climbing some steps. It was an
unpromising situation – a north-facing slope with
heavy clay soil. The prominent tree just beyond the
back wall is *Acer pseudoplatanus* 'Brilliantissimum',
a striking sight with its pink-flushed leaves in early
spring. Beyond the far wall is David's garden. *Opposite
right* At the top of the steps was the kitchen garden,
which Valerie transformed with her raised alpine beds
and two alpine houses, seen here in spring.

Swan cruise round the Mediterranean (page 113), and she appeared as a guest presenter on Percy Thrower's 'Gardening Club' and, later, as a contestant on BBC Pebble Mill's 'The Garden Game' with, among others, Percy Picton (see page 50).

After 28 years at Waterperry, Valerie took a rather unexpected step – she married. She often told the story of how, in 1968, Sir David Scott, a widowed, retired diplomat was visiting the garden and, in the Alpine Nursery, pointed out *Gillenia trifoliata* to his companion. From the depths of the potting shed a voice was heard: 'You're the first person who has ever known that plant!' Since his retirement in 1947, David had lived at The Dower House, part of Boughton House in Northamptonshire, which belonged to his cousin, the 8th Duke of Buccleuch. (David told Valerie he lived in a semi-detached house outside Kettering, which was true – in a way.) Immediately after the marriage ceremony, in July 1970, Valerie and David were out in the garden weeding, although they later travelled on honeymoon to Japan, where Valerie had been invited to lecture. They met leading

nurserymen there, including Koichiro Wada, and managed to
bring back some 300 plants for the garden at The Dower House.

Valerie's years with David at Boughton were sublimely happy
ones. The Scotts entertained a constant stream of visitors, all of
whom had to pose for the camera (a compact one for this purpose).
The resulting portraits were pasted into a succession of handsome,
leather-bound albums from Smythson's – the local postman
appears on the cover of one – into which all visitors, grand and
humble, were encouraged to write comments and draw pictures.

David was actively gardening until well into his nineties, and
he and Valerie spent all the daylight hours in the garden, usually
accompanied by a pug dog. The care they took was prodigious,
but necessary with so many 'treasures', as Valerie called them.
They regularly exhibited Boughton-grown plants at the RHS
'Fortnightlies' at Vincent Square, as Valerie had done before from
Waterperry, travelling up to London in her Morris Minor, the
back and boot loaded with plants in clay pots, as well as a wicker
basket crammed with sandwiches, cake and thermos flasks.

Opposite Magnolia x *wieseneri* (syn. *M.* x *watsonii*)
and *Helleborus* x *sternii* 'Boughton Beauty'. *Above*
Ken Aslet, Superintendent of the Rock Garden at
Wisley, walking by the RHS Old Hall in Vincent
Square, London. Valerie's Morris Minor is being
unloaded, with pots for an AGS show on the
pavement; in the front is pink *Phlox adsurgens*.

In 1983, David's health began to decline, and he died
in early August, 1986, just a few months short of his 100th
birthday. The following March, Valerie held a birthday
party to celebrate what would have been his centenary,
inviting a lively mixture of his old friends, including his
GP, the stonemason who made his memorial in the garden,
at least one duke and one former prime minister, not to
mention a scatter of explorers, ambassadors, peers of the
realm and writers. It was a tribute to David's particular
charm and sweetness of character, his natural distinction,
his ability to get on with everybody, his ready wit, and his
broad sympathies. He was a truly lovable man, a 'verray
parfit gentil knyght'.

In 1990, Valerie founded The Merlin Trust, named after
Sir David's only son, who had been killed in North Africa
in 1941. This provides travel scholarships for young,
aspiring and adventurous horticulturists. Many prominent
gardeners, such as Tom Hart Dyke, were helped in this way,
and Valerie, as Secretary for a number of years, always took
a close interest in all 'my Merlins', keeping tabs on them in
their future careers.

In later life, Valerie remained at The Dower House,
although she was on RHS committees until 2002 and,
each May, was coaxed up to London to the Chelsea Flower
Show, which she attended for more than fifty years. Her
health declined, but her spirit remained strong, and she
retained her puckish sense of humour to the last. She died,
after a short illness, on 17 October, 2006, at the age of 81.

David, like all good gardeners, spent most of his time in the garden on his knees,
here with Kate, the pug. His 2-acre garden, with trees, shrubs and groundcovering
perennials in beds connected by winding grass paths, was a delight at every season.

I

THE EDUCATION
OF A GARDENER

Students at Waterperry training a fan peach tree,
Peregrine, against a wall. Note the raffia used for
tying in the shoots; every task at Waterperry had
to be done with the greatest care.

Valerie's position as a woman professional gardener in the mid-twentieth century is an interesting one. From the very beginning of the century, when Frances Wolseley founded the Glynde School for Lady Gardeners (1902) and Lady Warwick her Studley College (1903), there had been a recognition that women were perfectly capable of being good gardeners, and that they should be given the opportunity. And not just any women, but often privately educated, upper-middle-class girls, such as Valerie.

These were the clientele of the school of horticulture founded by Miss Beatrix Havergal and Miss Avice Sanders in 1932 and based at Waterperry House in Oxfordshire, which Valerie was to join in 1942. Miss Havergal had worked at Downe House (a school, coincidentally, that Valerie attended), and had struck up a close friendship with Avice Sanders, the housekeeper there. In 1927, they set up a small school for women gardeners in the rented gardener's cottage and walled garden of Pusey House,

Opposite, clockwise Waterperry students in the frame yard; *Chrysanthemum*; students in the cucumber house in the 1950s; *Papaver orientale* 'Mrs Perry'; Valerie and student in the Alpine Nursery; *Meconopsis betonicifolia*, the legendary Himalayan blue poppy.
Right Anagallis 'Waterperry Pink' and *Clematis* 'Bill MacKenzie', a chance seedling named by Valerie after 'my great friend and mentor', Bill MacKenzie, Curator of the Chelsea Physic Garden.

near Faringdon in Oxfordshire. It was a great success, and in 1932 the demand for places forced them to look for larger premises. Waterperry, with its house and estate, seemed suitable. It was leased initially from Magdalen College, Oxford, but the opportunity arose in 1948 to buy it outright. On around 38 acres of land (another 42 acres were taken up with agriculture), young women were trained in the commercial production of horticultural crops, as well as 'private methods' – what we would call amenity horticulture. There were glasshouses and frames, orchards, an extensive soft-fruit area, walled gardens, flower garden, herbaceous plant nursery and, under Valerie's care, an alpine nursery.

The thorough – and by today's standards very rigorous – training that Miss Havergal instituted at the Waterperry Horticultural School for Women was a mixture of practical and theoretical education, lasting for two years. Emphasis was very much on the practical; standards were staggeringly high and the work was carried out with a neat and orderly efficiency that would have gladdened the heart of a Victorian martinet head gardener. It demanded a great deal both of the female students and the staff, although the regime was essentially kindly and Christian.

By example and sheer force of personality Miss Havergal inspired her staff and students to accept

Left (top to bottom) Potting up rooted cuttings of Kabschia saxifrages; students taking a practical exam; planting cuttings in a cold frame; Valerie teaching school children in the Alpine Nursery. *Opposite* Alpine Nursery cuttings frame (*above*); Miss Havergal and student planting seedlings from clay pots, with Ben, Miss H's golden retriever, in attendance (*below*). Note the quality of the fruit bushes growing on the wall behind.

without question a Spartan regime, with work starting at 7 a.m.,
winter and summer, no tea breaks, and no question of payment
for overtime. The spirit of the whole place indeed was such that
it never occurred to anybody employed there that this was not
a perfectly normal way of working.

There are photographs of a line of students double-digging
(perhaps the hardest gardening job there is), for example, and
Valerie remembered having to stoke the greenhouse coke boilers
early on winter mornings, a terrible task and, surely, a recipe for
aches and pains in old age. 'We used to faint in the sulphur fumes
sometimes, pulling out the clinkers' she told Nigel Colborn in

1988. 'If you woke at two in the morning and weren't sure whether you'd put the boiler's damper in, you had to light your hurricane lamp and go down to make sure.' Although a few men were employed at Waterperry, the girls were not spared the heaviest tasks and Valerie remembered driving the grey Ferguson ('Fergie') tractor. They wore a uniform of white, short-sleeved shirts, green dungarees and stout shoes in summer, and tweed jackets and breeches in winter; it was practical, if not exactly elegant, but Valerie continued to wear it even when she became a member of the teaching and working staff in 1944.

During the Second World War, the Waterperry 'girls' did their bit for the nation, producing vegetables, flowers and fruit to sell in the market in Oxford, and the School trained Land Girls as well. Valerie recalled delivering produce on her bicycle to Oxford colleges such as Keble. A shop was opened in the covered market

Opposite Miss Havergal lecturing at Waterperry on a sunny summer's day. *Above left* A class photograph of Waterperry staff and students, possibly in 1955. The 'redoubtable' Miss H, without a hat for a change, is seated in the middle of the second row and (*above right*) talks to a visitor at Waterperry.

in the town in the early part of the war, which became very popular and successful, especially when it moved to a prime site in 1949. Valerie had the task of driving a three-ton lorry in summer, carrying soft fruit to the market at Covent Garden in London, which meant leaving Waterperry at 4 a.m., or even earlier.

Miss Havergal was very keen on fruit-growing, and her great day came every May at the Chelsea Flower Show when she presided, a majestic if somewhat eccentric figure, over the stand of the famous Waterperry strain of 'Royal Sovereign' strawberries, every berry of which, whatever the weather had been, was invariably in perfect condition. The doyenne of the strawberry growing was

Right A Chelsea Gold Medal winning exhibit of 'Royal Sovereign' strawberries with Miss Havergal and students. *Above* Miss Joan Stokes (who was awarded the Veitch Memorial Medal) forced the strawberries into early fruit in the greenhouse.

Joan Stokes, a diminutive but obviously highly energetic and
skilled gardener, who had come to Waterperry as a student and
stayed on to work in the glasshouses (and looked after Miss
Havergal in her retirement). These strawberries were 'forced'
into early flower and fruit in the greenhouses and were of
superlative quality. The first small exhibit was in 1938; after the
Second World War exhibits expanded substantially: 300 plants
were arranged in great pyramids of green and glistening red. The
first Gold came in 1955 and there were to be 15 awarded in the 16
years until 1970, the last time they were staged, just a year before
the school closed. It was the custom for the stand to be visited by
the Royal party in their perambulation round the show, and for
a consignment of the fruit to be sent to Buckingham Palace.

   In 1960, Miss Havergal was appointed MBE and in 1966
she was awarded the VMH, the Victoria Medal of Honour, the
highest award that the Royal Horticultural Society can offer, and
one that Valerie herself was to win some nine years later. But, by
then, the demand for this kind of education for well-brought-up
ladies was declining. Indeed, by 1958, they were already having

Above Valerie also photographed arrangements of fruits and vegetables – sometimes quite
surreal. Here are strawberries, mixed vegetables and a basket of berries and cherries.
Opposite A hardy Waterperry student, in short sleeves, digging in frosty weather; snow
blankets the pots in a cold frame, with only the labels showing.

difficulty filling the spaces (26 was the maximum possible) because of rising costs and the lack of grants available to help students pay the fees. It may also have had something to do with changes in society at large – the drab post-war years of austerity were over and the Sixties were about to swing. Although only a few miles from Oxford, the students could not get there often, and boyfriends were definitely not encouraged. It was a firm feminocracy – which might also have put off some doting parents.

In 1971, the school was sold to the School of Economic Science and the Waterperry Horticultural School ceased to exist (Studley College had folded shortly before). Fortunately, the staff were kept on and the gardens have continued to flourish. Courses of a rural, horticultural or craft nature are taught there and there is an art gallery and museum, as well as an annual arts festival. The National Collection of Kabschia and Engleria saxifrages is housed there, a direct result of Valerie's enduring influence, of course.

Miss Havergal, who was given a cottage in Waterperry in which
to live, died in 1980; in an affectionate obituary published in
The Times, Sir David Scott, Valerie's husband, wrote: 'Kindly
and benevolent, Miss Havergal was yet a redoubtable figure
who dominated her surroundings and would have stood out
in any company, dressed as she invariably was in a green linen
smock surmounted by a dark green blazer, with green breeches
and green wool stockings, a white shirt and brown tie, and a dark
brown hat.'

A number of very successful Waterperry graduates maintained
the finest traditions of the School as employed gardeners around
the country, including Susan Dickinson, presently at Eythrop, a
very private Rothschild garden looked after to the highest
standards. Pamela Schwerdt and Sibylle Kreutzberger, Waterperry
students in the 1950s, were employed by Vita Sackville-West at
Sissinghurst Castle in Kent in 1959. It was perhaps an intimidating
job to begin with: in an interview in 2006 they said that 'when we
first went to Sissinghurst, people used to point at us as though we
were baboons at the zoo'. Because they had worked closely with
Vita before her death in 1962, they could continue to nurture her
unique garden, following her precepts, after the National Trust
took it over. The Sissinghurst 'girls' had a reputation for prodigious
skill, flair and hard work – all good Waterperry virtues – which
they have continued in their own garden, now they are retired,
in Gloucestershire.

In the 1950s, when Valerie took up her camera, professional
horticulture was in a state of rapid, if not readily acknowledged,
change. What was still often called 'private service' was in slow
decline, the victim not only of two extremely disruptive and
lengthy world wars but also of an increasingly democratically
inclined population, which no longer wanted to be considered
as 'servants'. The hierarchical nature of horticultural employment,

Sibylle Kreutzberger and Pamela Schwerdt, wheeling
sturdy wooden barrows, were hired at Sissinghurst
Castle in 1959 by Vita Sackville-West, later becoming
joint Head Gardeners. They both studied at
Waterperry in Valerie's time.

with its steady progression from 'boy' to head gardener, established in the Victorian era, was not as attractive as it had once been. Many landowners and owners of large gardens did themselves or their gardeners no favours, it is true. In particular, there was a widespread refusal to remunerate gardeners generously – in 1945, a single-handed gardener earned £3/10/6d a week; the accommodation was tied, and there was a frequent requirement that an applicant's wife work in the house as a cleaner, and that there be no children. Only very traditional – old-fashioned even – gardeners had no qualms about that.

This decline can be traced in the pages of gardening newspapers, in particular *The Gardeners' Chronicle*, a weekly paper in which most situations in the gardening world, vacant and wanted, were posted. A typical advertisement from someone seeking a position would read: 'Head Gardener, where some staff

Above left Saxifraga 'Cranbourne'; *above right* A group in Alan Bloom's garden at Bressingham, Norfolk: Flora Bloom, Adrian Bloom, Fred Whitsey, Alan Bloom, Sir David Scott and Arthur Shackleton. *Opposite* Jack Drake, in his Inshriach Nursery near Aviemore in Scotland, with sugar-pink *Lewisia cotyledon* in the foreground.

employed. Lord [......] recommends his Head Gardener. Life
experience inside and out in first-class establishments.' By 1955,
there were three times as many situations Vacant as Wanted.
Increasingly, private estates turned to market gardening as a way
of recouping some of the costs of labour and to find an outlet
for surplus produce as servant numbers plummeted, although
this was rarely a resounding success. The final blow came with
the oil crisis of 1973, and its associated inflation, when many
garden owners were forced to close down greenhouse boilers
and lay off staff for good.

One consequence, however, was that garden owners
themselves became more 'hands-on', and a number became
first-class cultivators and plantsmen as a result, as we shall see in
the next chapter. And perhaps the traditional conservatism of
professional 'private service' gardeners had had its day – it was
not always to the employer's advantage, after all. The inverted
balance of power between the anxious and sometimes

Opposite left Will Ingwersen in his nursery at Birch Farm, Sussex, founded by his father, Walter. A stalwart of RHS committees, he was the only person ever permitted to smoke in the RHS Library. *Opposite right* Another nurseryman, Arthur Branch, inspecting his cold frames in his alpine nursery at Shipton-on-Cherwell, Oxfordshire.

Above A great expert on alpines, Clarence Elliott founded Six Hills Nursery in Stevenage in 1907, from whence emanated many new and wonderful alpine and perennial plants. He was an innovative grower, popularizing the use of stone troughs for miniature alpine gardens, and was a major influence on Valerie and other alpine growers.

The chess-set topiary in Nancy Lancaster's garden
at Haseley Court, with its Alice in Wonderland feel.
Mr Shepherd (*above*), whom Valerie called 'This dear
wonderful old man', continued to clip the chess set with
his hand shears, even during the Second World War, when
he had officially retired.

deferential Lord Emsworth and his fearsome Scottish gardener, McAllister, in P. G. Wodehouse's Blandings stories, although an obvious caricature, had its basis in fact.

Despite the success of Waterperry and other establishments like it, many head gardeners, and their employers, still considered that gardening was man's work – until comparatively recently. For example, those women who worked in the Shrewsbury Parks Department during the Second World War were replaced by men when Percy Thrower went there as Superintendent in 1946. It was probably not until the 1970s that there was a growing understanding that there was little that women could not do and, moreover, in nursery propagation work, for example, their care and nimble fingers might actually make them superior to men.

Valerie Finnis was a professional gardener, of course, with a number of 'old school' gardeners as friends or acquaintances, and she often photographed them at work in their nurseries and gardens or at the Chelsea Flower Show. Amongst these was Fred Nutbeam, Head Gardener at Buckingham Palace between 1954 and 1978, and also Mr Shepherd who, though retired, kept the famous chess-set topiary ('my Kings and Queens') clipped at Haseley Court throughout the Second World War, when the house was occupied by the American forces and the garden otherwise neglected. Valerie considered Bill (W. G.) MacKenzie, the Scottish-born Curator of the Chelsea Physic Garden in London from 1946 to 1973, to be 'my great friend and mentor'. He gave Valerie useful advice about staging exhibits, and it was after him that she named the fine hybrid of the autumn-flowering 'orange-peel' clematis (a cross between *Clematis orientalis* and *C. tangutica*), which he had spotted as a self-sown seedling in the Alpine Nursery at Waterperry (see page 25).

This was also a time when gardening became a hobby for growing numbers of householders without walled gardens or landed estates, and the desire for information about it also grew. Before the war, knowledge about gardening for the amateur came from books, magazines and, increasingly, the broadcast media. C. H Middleton started to broadcast on the wireless in the 1930s and, in 1947, came 'How does your Garden Grow?' with Fred Loads and Bill Sowerbutts on BBC's Home Service. In 1950, this became 'Gardeners' Question Time', when Professor Alan Gemmell joined the team. 'Gardeners' Question Time' has survived pretty well intact to the present day on Radio 4, the name given to the Home Service after 1967.

Fred Nutbeam, who was the Head Gardener at Buckingham Palace for a quarter of a century and definitely of the 'Old School'.

Geoffrey Smith started at the Northern Horticultural Society's new garden at Harlow Carr, Harrogate, in 1954, laying out the garden and supervising it until he left in 1974. He then had a successful career in television, with 'Mr Smith's Flowers' as well as other shows.

Opposite The dapper Percy Thrower, the first television gardener, at a Chelsea Flower Show with Ken Burras, Curator of the Oxford Botanic Gardens. The best-known British gardener for many years – his television career extended from 1952 to 1976 – Thrower also revived the Shrewsbury Flower Show and owned one of the first garden centres in Britain.

Television now also turned the media spotlight on gardening: Percy Thrower became a household name because of 'Gardening Club' – on which Valerie was a guest presenter – the programme which was the precursor to the BBC's 'Gardeners' World'. Thrower became a businessman, too, buying the old Murrells nursery just outside Shrewsbury, with a partner, in the 1970s, and starting a garden centre there. He was clearly a shrewd individual, who could see which way the wind was blowing.

Nurserymen in America had begun growing plants in tin cans before the Second World War, and the idea began to spread

across the Atlantic to Great Britain. An early experimenter was
Waterers, the tree and shrub nursery in Bagshot, Surrey. But, in
the immediate post-war years, almost all plant nurseries,
whether wholesale or retail, continued to sell plants grown
on site. These were, in the case of hardy plants at least, usually
field-grown, as with Mr Mattock and his roses, and lifted in
the dormant season. The revolution was on its way, however.
When plastic containers began to be mass-produced in the 1960s,
garden centre retail outlets – as opposed to nurseries – rapidly
gained in popularity. People could visit and pick up plants as
in any other shop and, a great advantage, container-grown
plants could be planted all year round, within reason. Garden
centres, and their products, seemed to require much less skill

Opposite Rose 'Paul's Scarlet Climber', a fine cultivar.
Above Graham Stuart Thomas was a nurseryman,
prolific author and Gardens Adviser to the National
Trust. One of his particular interests was Old Roses.
He told Valerie that his enthusiasm for roses began
as a child: 'I was brought up with 'Mrs John Laing'
and 'Alister Stella Gray' and other famous varieties
and I remember at the age of, well, about fifteen,
I should think, I started buying a few roses.'

Valerie caught the glowing colours of roses with
great skill (*clockwise from top left*): Rose
'Masquerade'; an unknown rose; Rose
'Frühlingsmorgen'; Rose 'Ena Harkness'.

John W. Mattock, a famous Oxfordshire rose
nurseryman, standing among his field-grown roses,
with a freshly cut bouquet – perhaps for Valerie –
raffia dangling from his jacket ready for use.

and knowledge on the part of the gardening public (and staff),
although, in mitigation it has to be said that they were not the
daunting places for novices that old-style family-run nurseries
could be. These developments were viewed with some suspicion
by Valerie and her circle, since the garden centre seemed to bring
with it a rise of expectations but, at the same time, a dumbing-
down in horticultural skills. And they may well have been right:
certainly, it seems more than coincidence that after Sir Harold
Hillier's death in 1985 the nursery abandoned mail order for
direct selling through garden centres and the famous Hilliers'
plant list shrank dramatically.

Valerie counted many specialist nurserymen amongst her
friends. And many of them grew alpine plants in particular
– not surprisingly given Valerie's interests. They included the
much-admired alpine nurseryman, Jack Drake (see page 37),
at Inshriach near Aviemore in the Highlands, as well as Stuart
Boothman, who helped found the Alpine Garden Society and

In Valerie's time many of the great nurseries were family-run affairs. On the left is Percy Picton
and his son Paul, admiring a rock bed at Old Court Nursery in Colwall, Worcestershire; Percy
and Valerie appeared on TV programmes together. On the right is Will Ingwersen, son of
Walter, with his brother Paul.

Stuart Boothman, another alpine specialist
nurseryman, from Maidenhead, with one of Valerie's
godchildren, Barnaby Newbolt, helping out. Valerie
always enjoyed the company of children and young
people and a clutch of godchildren benefited greatly
from her attention.

had a nursery at Furze Platt, Maidenhead, in Berkshire, and Joe Elliott, the son of Clarence, who had an alpine nursery at Broadwell in Gloucestershire. Many nursery businesses passed from father to son; for instance, Will Ingwersen took on Birch Farm nursery at Gravetye from his father, the famous Walter, and was followed by his brother Paul, while Paul Picton took on his father Percy's Michaelmas daisy nursery. Valerie's friendship with Sir Harold Hillier may well have flourished after her marriage to David, since he had bought rare trees and shrubs from the Hampshire nursery for many years.

The Royal Horticultural Society is an organization dedicated to educating and enlightening amateur gardeners – by example in the gardens it owns, by the journal it produces, as well as by the flower shows it stages. It has been the power in the horticultural land in Britain for the past two hundred years. Founded in 1804 as the Horticultural Society of London, but changing its name in 1861, it currently has some 370,000 members. In Valerie's heyday, it was much, much smaller, rather aristocratic in atmosphere and

Left The Chelsea Flower Show in late May is the highlight of the horticultural year in Britain; Queen Elizabeth II (in the centre, in shadow) takes a great interest, as did the Queen Mother. *Opposite* Harold Hillier, the finest tree and shrub nurseryman of his generation, puts the finishing touches to an exhibit at Chelsea. The amount of care and effort that went into these show gardens was phenomenal – for just four days of public viewing.

the members were still called 'Fellows'. The big events were the 'fortnightly' shows held at the Society's headquarters in Vincent Square (in the Old and New Halls, now the Lindley and Lawrence Halls), as well as the Chelsea Flower Show, held in the grounds of the Royal Hospital in Chelsea since 1913. From 1903, it also owned one garden, close to the A3 in Surrey, at Wisley (where the first women gardeners were employed in 1917). There are now also RHS gardens at Rosemoor in Devon, Hyde Hall in Essex and Harlow Carr in Yorkshire. The main branch of the world-famous Lindley Library is housed in Vincent Square.

Presidents of the RHS in Valerie's time tended to be garden-minded grandees: the 2nd Baron Aberconway of Bodnant, North Wales (President 1931–53); Sir David Bowes-Lyon (1953–61), the brother of Queen Elizabeth, the Queen Mother, who had a garden at St Paul's Walden Bury in Hertfordshire; and then the 3rd Baron Aberconway, also of Bodnant (1961–84). Valerie certainly knew the last two well.

The Society has a rich variety of awards to offer to meritorious gardeners, the most prestigious of which is the Victoria Medal of Honour; there can only ever be 63 living recipients – one for every year of Queen Victoria's reign. Valerie received the VMH in 1975, and no other award gave her more, and more justifiable, pleasure. It was recognition of her outstanding contribution both to the cultivation of alpine plants and to garden photography.

A rock garden exhibit at Chelsea by Wisley Gardens, in 1968, though it is hard to believe that this is a temporary garden. Christopher Brickell, then botanist at Wisley, is checking labels, while Ken Aslet, Superintendent of the Rock Garden and a great friend of Valerie's, looks on.

J. L. Russell at Chelsea, taking a rest and checking his
notes seated on black plastic sacks, full of soil or peat,
no doubt. *Opposite* Experts judging alpines at an
RHS show in Vincent Square. Much of the work
of the RHS is done by dedicated expert volunteers
such as these. This prestigious group includes David
Shackleton, the Irish alpine enthusiast and great
friend of Valerie (on the left), with Sir Frederick Stern
(third from left), E. B. Anderson to his left and (half-
hidden) R. B. Cooke, a fine amateur plantsman.

Valerie served on at least two RHS committees: the rather intriguingly named – to the uninitiated at least – Joint Rock (1962–82) and also Floral 'B' (trees and shrubs; 1972–2002). At the same time she was showing new plants (mainly good selections of existing ones) that she had developed, a number of which gained horticultural awards such as Cultural Commendations, the Award of Merit and, best of all, the First Class Certificate. Among Valerie's plants still in nursery catalogues are *Helleborus* x *sternii* 'Boughton Beauty', *Hepatica transsilvanica* 'Ada Scott' (named after David's mother), *Artemisia ludoviciana* 'Valerie Finnis', *Artemisia stelleriana* 'Boughton Silver', *Hebe cupressoides* 'Boughton Dome' and the vibrant powder-blue *Muscari armeniacum* 'Valerie Finnis'.

II

COUNTRY HOUSE
& COTTAGE GARDEN

Margery Fish, with her back to the camera, talking
to Mr and Mrs Gerard Parker (see page 119), in
her garden at East Lambrook Manor in Somerset.
A tour of the ¾-acre garden with her could take up
to five hours!

The gradual decline in the availability of skilled labour following the Second World War had profound effects on garden design, but one very positive outcome was that many garden owners began to become more directly involved. A number of Valerie's photographs are of gentry who happily got their hands dirty: Lewis Palmer, Nancy Lancaster, Rhoda Birley and Vita Sackville-West. Of course, this had always been the case to a certain extent, but the trend undoubtedly became more marked. The middle classes also continued to embrace practical gardening, especially when they had the opportunity to buy house and gardens outside the big cities. One of the best documented of these gardens, because its owner was a firm friend of Valerie's and was herself a prolific gardening writer, was East Lambrook Manor in Somerset. It belonged to Margery Fish who, with her husband, Walter Fish, editor of the *Daily Mail*, bought the house in 1937.

Opposite and overleaf Margery Fish – who always seems to have gardened in a dress, at least in Valerie's photographs of her – was the most famous exponent of the Cottage Garden ideal at this period. She wrote: 'Plants are friendly creatures and enjoy each other's company. The close-packed plants in a cottage garden grow well and look happy.' *Right* Typical cottage garden plants: *Primula vulgaris*, the primrose, and *Selinum carvifolium; page 62* Solomon's Seal, *Polygonatum multiflorum.*

Although she died in 1969, Margery Fish is still a revered
figure in British horticulture; Valerie's photographs of her have
done much to preserve her image. Fish developed the idea of
the 'cottage garden', initially championed by Gertrude Jekyll
in late Victorian times. This was not the cottage garden as
Victorian cottagers knew it, in fact, but a more sophisticated,
plant-rich version. The jumble of hardy plants in informal
borders, with a rustic structure of hedges and a scattering
of fruit trees, was an old tradition revived, and many favourite
cottage garden plants were rescued from possible extinction

'Fish', as Valerie called her (at Waterperry the girls always called each other by their surnames and the habit lasted all her life), was decidedly a 'hands-on' gardener. She delighted in rediscovering old cottage garden favourite plants, and selecting promising self-sown seedlings or sports, such as the plant opposite, *Euphorbia* 'Lambrook Gold', named after her house and photographed by Valerie there.

in the process. Care was taken with siting them where they would flourish – 'the right plant in the right place' school of thought – and interesting, self-sown seedlings were noted and preserved. Brash colour, a feature of many rural gardens at the time, full of dahlias and chrysanthemums, was eschewed. This was gardening in shades of green, where interesting foliage was as important as flowers, and where sub-fusc hellebores, euphorbias and pulmonarias were treasured.

Margery Fish introduced to cultivation a number of excellent garden plants, nearly all of them grown as much for their leaves as their flowers. There is her famous *Astrantia major* 'Shaggy', and euphorbias, a *Lamium* (dead nettle), a penstemon and a pulmonaria all carry her name.

Vita Sackville-West, the châtelaine of Sissinghurst Castle
in Kent, now in the care of the National Trust, was another
champion of this style of gardening. Vita was married to Sir
Harold Nicolson, the diplomat and author, and they had bought
Sissinghurst in 1930. It is likely that Valerie met her towards the
end of her life (she died in 1962), after two Waterperry 'girls',
Pamela Schwerdt and Sibylle Kreutzberger, went to work for her.
The garden – as well as its owner – was unique, with the Tudor
tower where Vita had her writing room separated by a flowery
courtyard from the main living quarters, while she and her

Valerie took scarcely any pictures of gardens without people prominently in them, but she
probably enjoyed the striking contrast between floral profusion and the austere Tudor tower
at Sissinghurst Castle. Vita Sackville-West, the creator of the garden, is seen here (*above*)
inspecting urns at the base of the tower with Miss Havergal, Sibylle Kreutzberger and Pamela
Schwerdt – the Waterperry connection. *Page 69* An opulent still life of Old Shrub Roses.

husband actually slept in South Cottage, another building in the garden. Evident in Valerie's picture is the extraordinary personality of Vita herself, a woman memorably described by Noel Coward as 'Lady Chatterley above the waist and the gamekeeper below'.

Whether Vita influenced Margery Fish or vice versa, or there was a collective consciousness working at the time, is now difficult to say, but Sissinghurst, although on a much larger scale, is in some aspects similar to East Lambrook. There is a Cottage Garden, for example, in front of the South Cottage, where Vita put plants in what she called 'the sunset colours', and the intermingling of flowers, including many that had once been old favourites, was much in evidence in the borders. In Vita's case, however, shrubs, especially roses, were also a key element, especially the single-flowering Old Roses, which, by the Second World War, had been so successfully supplanted generally by repeat-flowering Hybrid Tea and Floribunda roses. Vita, together with Graham Stuart Thomas (see page 47) and E. A. Bunyard, must take a lot of the credit for rescuing many of these from obscurity and popularizing them once more. The garden at Boughton, too, is home to old and species roses, such as 'Golden Chersonese', thanks to David, and there used to be a beautiful, blood-red 'Guinée' on the south-facing wall of The Dower House.

In one respect the garden at Sissinghurst differed from that at East Lambrook Manor; it was much more strongly structured. This was thanks partly to the strenuous efforts of Sir Harold Nicolson, and was a response to the size of the garden. The idea of colour, profusion and botanical interest within a strong framework is one that has been popular for a century or more, since the early days of the Arts and Crafts garden, but it reached its apotheosis at Sissinghurst. And, thanks in part to the Waterperry 'girls', this has survived to the present.

Opposite The laburnum tunnel at Haseley Court,
with spider's web bench: Valerie took this
photograph standing in front of a mirror, which
made the tunnel look longer than it really was.
The arches also diminished in size – another optical
illusion employed to exaggerate the length. Nancy
Lancaster (*above and overleaf*), who created the
garden at Haseley, was a patrician Virginian and
niece of Nancy Astor. Although American, she was
a supremely successful exponent of the 'English
Country House Style'.

Another devotee of this kind of decorative, flower-rich gardening was Nancy Lancaster. For many years after 1954 she lived at Haseley Court in Little Haseley, only a short step from Wheatley, where Valerie lived. Haseley Court is famous for the chess-set topiary, laid out after 1850. After a disastrous fire in the house in 1970, Nancy sold the Court and moved into the nearby Coach House, but retained control of most of the garden. As a result of Valerie's good offices, I was taken on as a part-time gardener by Nancy Lancaster when I finished university in 1974. Because of the wonderful summer I spent there, a holiday job turned into the start of a career.

Nancy Lancaster had been a partner in the fashionable firm of interior decorators, Colefax and Fowler, promoting the relaxed English Country House style (despite being a patrician American from Virginia). And it was a relaxed country style that she pursued in the garden. Both structure and planting were equally sure (although, despite her own strong ideas, she did also consult Russell Page, Vernon Russell-Smith and Graham Stuart Thomas). Sophisticated half-hardy annuals such as *Nicotiana* 'Lime Green' were signature plants in the box-edged borders, as were the laburnum walk (see page 70), the goblet-shaped apple trees, the blue speedwell-spangled lawn and a hedge of *Rosa gallica* 'Versicolor' combined with pink, red and white sweet Williams. All the structures and ornaments in

the garden were both handsome and practical, in particular the
gazebo which formed the centre of four paths, and the white-
painted wooden benches which had wheels as well as legs, and
handles at one end, so that they could be moved easily on the lawn
when one mowed. Nancy was a frequent worker in the garden,
always followed by her elegant dogs.

Valerie's move to The Dower House widened her horticultural
circle, giving her the chance to get to know better one of the
foremost ecologists, conservationists and biologists of the century,
the Honourable Miriam Rothschild (later Dame Miriam), who
lived at Ashton Wold, near Oundle, not far from Boughton.
Rothschild's influence in promoting the idea of meadow gardening
– now so fashionable – in order to preserve wild flowers and the
native fauna which feeds on them, has been enormous.

Opposite Anemone pavonina (*left*) and wild flowers, including orchids (*right*), both in Greece, probably taken when Valerie was a guest lecturer on a Swan Hellenic cruise.

Dame Miriam Rothschild at her home at Ashton Wold in Northamptonshire. She was a noted scientist and a great conservation campaigner; Valerie described her as 'The greatest of all human beings and the kindest, the most courageous'. She showed that serving afternoon tea properly was compatible with daisies in the lawn.

Valerie had a knack of making friends with unusual, interesting people, but Miriam Rothschild must surely have been the most individual. Dressed usually in mauve frocks and headdresses, an outfit often completed, even on the grandest occasions, by white Wellingtons (she was a bee-keeper), she held a yearly party in early June. A varied collection of people, including Valerie, would be invited to have lunch and see what progress she was making in conservationist farming and the commercial production of wild flower seed. Her most famous mixture she called 'Farmer's Nightmare', a selection of annuals once common in cornfields but chased out by efficient herbicides. Miriam Rothschild numbered among her influential friends the Prince of Wales, for whom she made a meadow at Highgrove, Gloucestershire, and so the ecological word spread. Miriam and Valerie continued to keep in touch until extreme old age (Miriam died in 2005, at the age of 97).

John Codrington, a garden designer living at Hambleton, overlooking Rutland Water, was also a follower of a more eco-friendly kind of gardening. Indeed, he owned the garden before the valley below the village was flooded to make the reservoir,

Opposite John Codrington in his garden at Hambleton, overlooking Rutland Water, which he created on what were then thought to be ecological lines. Behind him is the giant hogweed (*Heracleum mantegazzianum*), which now has a rather sinister reputation as invasive and potentially harmful. He was a diplomat and probable spy who designed gardens in retirement, in England and abroad.
Left A wild umbellifer, perhaps the common cow parsley – tamer and safer than the giant hogweed.

so he had an interesting perspective on the different micro-
climate that resulted. A cultured, one-time diplomat and spy,
his garden was created very much on ecological lines, with wild
flowers interspersed amongst more cultivated kinds. 'My garden
is not a normal, civilized garden. It is a mad, wild jungle. …
It is full of weeds, which I call wild flowers.' There were times
when it could look a little out of control, but it was certainly
always full of interesting plants.

Codrington's garden was perhaps no more than half an acre
in extent. In contrast, Sir John and Lady Heathcoat Amory
were the owners and developers of a 12-acre garden at
Knightshayes Court in Devon (now belonging to the National
Trust), significant for its formal gardens, high-spirited topiary
and its collection of trees and shrubs, many of them rare and
tender, which thrived in the mild, wet Devon climate. So highly
regarded were they in the horticultural world that he received
the VMH in 1966 and she in 1981. Before she married, as Joyce
Wethered, Lady Heathcoat Amory had been a famous lady

The Heathcoat Amorys at Knightshayes Court
in Devon: after the Second World War the couple
developed the garden, first laid out in the 1890s,
and the surrounding woodland; it was acquired by
the National Trust in 1972. In his later years Sir John
used an electric chair to move around the garden,
but would frequently lose it after he got out to show
visitors around. Valerie affectionately recalled how
he always put weeds he had pulled up in his pocket.

golfer, winner of the Ladies' British Open Championship four
times. The legendary American golfer Bobby Jones maintained
that she was the greatest golfer – man or woman – that he had
ever seen.

Valerie met the celebrated children's author, Roald Dahl, and
his first wife, the Hollywood film star Patricia Neal, when they
visited Waterperry with their children, and there is a persistent
legend that Dahl modelled the dreaded 'Miss Trunchbull' in his
book *Matilda* on Miss Havergal. The Dahls lived at Great
Missenden in Buckinghamshire, and Valerie took a number of
photographs of them over the years. I remember, some time in
the 1990s, driving her to the Gipsy House, as it was called, to

Opposite Roald Dahl the world-famous author
of children's books, with two of his children, Theo
and Olivia, at the Gipsy House. *Above* Patricia Neal
the American actress, was Dahl's first wife, seen here
with their daughter Tessa. This must have been on
a different occasion from the picture opposite, in
spring, with Neal's hat perfectly matching the colour
and shape of the tulip flowers.

Above Mixed Old Shrub Roses; a trug with roses in front of Charleston Manor, Sussex, home to Rhoda, Lady Birley; *Paeonia* 'Black Pirate'. *Opposite* Rhoda, Lady Birley, in the garden at Charleston. Valerie had a weakness for outrageous hats, both wearing them herself and photographing others in them.

meet his widow, Felicity, and see the famous Writing Hut and Gipsy Caravan in the garden.

Among Valerie's more exotic photographic subjects was Rhoda, Lady Birley, the widow of Sir Oswald Birley, the artist and fashionable society portrait painter, who lived at Charleston Manor in Sussex. Before her marriage she was Rhoda Pike, an Irish beauty, whom Birley painted many times. She and her husband were great patrons of the arts and held a festival at Charleston annually (which still takes place, usually in June), at which Valerie lectured. Rhoda Birley created a fine, idyllic garden, in the formal 'garden room' style, and Valerie's picture of her with parrot-bill loppers in hand bespeaks a highly practical approach.

Maurice Mason was a somewhat more down-to-earth subject for Valerie's camera, a farmer of Fincham in Norfolk. But he was also an avid grower of greenhouse plants, especially those for the 'stove', that is tropical plants – at one time he had 18 glasshouses. A great luminary of the Royal Horticultural Society, he chaired the Floral 'C' Committee for some years. He was also the last of the great amateur exhibitors at Chelsea – those non-commercial gardeners with sufficient resources to put on displays. He finally gave up only in the early 1980s. An avid collector of variegated begonias in particular, he is commemorated in *Begonia masoniana*.

In Valerie's younger days she travelled widely around Europe, most particularly to Germany to see Wilhelm Schacht (see the next chapter), but she also went to the south of France, to Norah Warre's garden at the Villa Rocquebrune (page 124) and to Miss Maybud

Campbell's at Val Rahmeh in Menton. Maybud Campbell had once been a concert singer, but when Valerie knew her she was a keen amateur botanist and, for a time, secretary of the Botanical Society of the British Isles (she published a *Flora of Uig*, making an annual botanical trip to the Outer Hebrides).

Val Rahmeh was a villa with a garden originally developed by Lord Radcliffe, governor of Malta, in the early twentieth century. It was bought and expanded by Maybud in 1957 and she planted many sub-tropical plants there. In 1966 she gave it over to the French National Museum of Natural History, and it is now a research centre concentrating on the Mediterranean flora. Maybud, despite her delicate-sounding name, had

a mercurial personality and was referred to by Valerie as 'a thorn in everyone's side'.

One of the many fascinating aspects of Valerie's photographic portraits of garden owners is what clothes they thought appropriate for wearing, and working, in the garden. Valerie and David were early devotees of the Husky, a padded jacket which kept them warm outside in winter. But then Valerie had always been a professional gardener and the masculine garb adopted at Waterperry was certainly very practical. Valerie also always wore trousers when working, though it is obvious from these photographs that some of her female contemporaries preferred to do their gardening in skirts, admittedly sensible tweed skirts capable of taking considerable wear and tear. The men, too, wear sturdy suits and gaberdine macintoshes. Or perhaps this was just Sunday luncheon wear, and Valerie caught them on film as they dug up a plant for her to take away with her after a visit? Others, such as 'Parsley' Mure, however, are

Page 84 Richard Grove Annesley made a garden at his home, Annes Grove in County Cork, Eire, with native and exotic species combined in a natural setting. He was an expert on rhododendrons – *above* are, possibly, 'Temple Belle' and *Rhododendron ferrugineum*, the Alpenrose. *Page 85* Maurice Mason, a farmer in Norfolk and avid cultivator and collector of tropical plants – Valerie remarked that he had 'a dog permanently on his shoulder'.

Opposite Maybud Campbell (*left*), a botanist and gardener at Menton, France, and Ruby Fleishmann (*right*), a great rose grower, with a particular interest in old French varieties, seen here in her second garden at Batsford, Gloucestershire. *Above* Adwell House in Oxfordshire, not far from Waterperry, and Mrs Birch Reynardson with son (presumably) and terrier (inevitably).

captured wearing impossibly glamorous outfits to carry out
their mundane garden tasks. Either way, these pictures capture
an era which seems rather hazy to us now. Distance certainly
lends enchantment.

Valerie's pictures also show how important dogs were to
these gardeners. There is the odd pug, but terriers of all shapes
and sizes are definitely the pet of choice. Perhaps they too
were dragooned by Valerie into the picture (it was always very
hard to refuse her photographic requests), but I think it more
likely they naturally accompanied their owners in the many
hours they spent in their gardens. For these were the real
enthusiasts.

Cecily 'Parsley' Mure (also opposite, with Joan
Seddon in yellow), in her garden in Buckingham
Palace Mews, London. She was presumably known
as 'Parsley' after the Beatrix Potter character Cecily
Parsley. Valerie remembered her as a 'brilliant
London gardener' and that the elegant dress she
wore to water her alpine trough on this occasion
was made of silk.

Many of the garden owners Valerie knew and photographed –
and including Valerie and David themselves – would have opened
their gardens to the public on certain days each year for the
National Gardens Scheme, a charitable endeavour that has had
a considerable impact on English gardening life, particularly since
the Second World War. The original gardens scheme was founded
to help provide pensions for district nurses and in its first year,
1927, more than 600 gardens opened and £8,191 was raised. For
many years visitors were charged a shilling a head – Vita Sackville-
West referred to her visitors on these occasions as 'the shillingses'.
Today, the Scheme can boast the support of 3,500 private and
public gardens – from the very grand to suburban back gardens –
in England and Wales, each opening at least one day a year.
Beneficiaries now include cancer and nursing charities, the
Gardeners' Royal Benevolent Society ('Perennial') and the
Royal Gardeners' Orphan Fund, as well as National Trust
trainee gardeners. There is a similar, if proportionately smaller,
organization in Scotland.

Opposite Mrs Frazer (Vera) Mackie (*left*), who gardened at Guincho, east of Belfast in Northern Ireland. This was a plantsman's garden, full of rare and choice plants. She had one large patch devoted entirely to the American trout lily, *Erythronium revolutum*. J. Brunskill (*right*) was another gardener, but someone about whom little has been discovered. Both gardened with dogs closely in attendance.

Ruth McConnel, who lived at Castle Hill, Farnham, grew *Rhodohypoxis* – a difficult genus from South Africa – extremely well, and showed wonderful displays at Chelsea, where Valerie got to know her. Valerie grew 17 varieties herself, inherited from the McConnel collection. Despite the fact that these plants are rather precious, the Maltese terrier is allowed to lie amongst them – in fact McConnel named a white variety, 'Perle', after this dog.

The NGS open days at The Dower House, Boughton,
in the 1970s and early 1980s were festival events, regularly seeing
1,200 visitors, and enabling Valerie and David to send a cheque
for £3,000 each year to the Scheme. This success was in part
because of the spectacularly popular plant sale held at the same
time. Most of the plants were propagated by David, who would
spend the summer working in the outdoor potting shed in the
Hawk Yard (where he had kept falcons as a boy), and in
a downstairs room in the house when the weather was cold.

The queues of people would begin to form an hour at least before
the garden officially opened after lunch on a summer Sunday, and
it was not uncommon for visitors to drive a hundred miles to see
the garden and buy plants from two such famous plantsmen.
I myself helped on several occasions and it was a nerve-wracking
business, since most of the plants were growing in small pots and
were unlabelled, or labelled only with the species name. It was,
on the other hand, a great gardeners' day out, since other helpers
included Dr Martyn Rix, botanist at Wisley, bulb expert and now
a well-known author, as well as Robin and Joan Grout, who were
great luminaries of the Hardy Plant Society, and Netta Statham,
a renowned plantsman from Shropshire, whose name lives on in
Viola cornuta 'Netta Statham' and *Pulmonaria* 'Netta Statham'.

The National Garden Scheme provides an outlet for many
private individuals to realize their charitable intentions and their
desire to share their gardens – these are people who could not,
or would not, contemplate opening them for financial gain. There
are, however, also large open gardens which give a day's takings to
the National Gardens Scheme and prominent among them are

David Scott with Jenny Robinson in her garden at Boxford in Suffolk. A plantswoman of
considerable note, her interests include iris and grape hyacinth (*Muscari*).

Above Richard (Dick) Trotter, who was Treasurer
of the RHS on several occasions, seen here in his
garden at Brin House, Inverness-shire, where he
lived when retired. His name is remembered in
various bulbs, including a snowdrop.
Opposite Netta Statham used to help Valerie and
David at the annual charity plant sales at The Dower
House. Several plants including a pulmonaria are
named after her.

those of the National Trust, an organization which is itself
a beneficiary of the Scheme. The post-war period was also
notable for the first opening to the public of a great number
of stately homes and large houses, for commercial rather than
charitable reasons. Many of these – Longleat, Woburn Abbey,
Charlecote Park, for example – also have important gardens or
landscapes. Valerie seems never to have been interested in taking
pictures of entire gardens, or even specific parts of them, being
more usually captivated by individual flowers, or groupings of
flowers, and, of course, their owners. Their gardens or plants
often seem to be inseparable from their personalities – or is that
just how Valerie showed them?

III

A PASSION FOR PLANTS

Norman Hadden, in his garden at Porlock in
Somerset, seen through a haze of Angel's Fishing
Rods (*Dierama pulcherrimum*). One of the old school
of gentlemen plantsmen, he is best remembered in
the dogwood *Cornus* 'Norman Hadden'.

Looking back now, it is easy to see that the 1950s and 1960s were a golden age for the 'plantsman' (the name for both man and woman in those days). Gardens were generally shrinking in size, so particular groups of plants, especially alpines, were increasingly cultivated as individual specimens, rather than as constituents of a large garden laid out according to design principles. Valerie would spend her spare time, when she was not travelling, lecturing or judging, visiting like-minded enthusiasts such as Amy Doncaster at Chandlers Ford in Hampshire, and Primrose Warburg, the widow of the great botanist, Dr Warburg, at Boar's Hill, just outside Oxford, Oliver Wyatt who owned a prep school called Maidwell Hall in Northamptonshire, or Eliot Hodgkin, who had a garden near Twyford in Berkshire.

There was something rather stately about the way these enthusiasts met in those days. Kath Dryden, a great specialist and exhibitor of alpine plants, recalls being taken to see

Opposite Primrose Warburg and Amy Doncaster, wielding a fork, in Valerie's Alpine Nursery at Waterperry, some time in the 1960s. *Right* The foxglove *Digitalis lanata* and a trillium, sometimes known as 'wake-robin'.

Clifford Crook's garden in the early 1960s: 'In those days one was always *taken* to see people'. I remember, too, as a young aspiring gardener in the mid-1970s, being introduced to plantsmen, who were kindly and took great pains to respond to a genuine interest, and from whom one rarely came away empty-handed. Valerie, herself, was very much of this tradition, being very generous with plants and information if she sensed a glimmer of enthusiasm.

One of the most remarkable plantsmen of the post-war period, whom Valerie knew and photographed, was the Hon. Lewis Palmer, a younger son of the Earl of Selborne, who gardened for many years on a chalk soil near Winchester, at Headbourne Worthy. He was the first person seriously to hybridize agapanthus, and developed the famous 'Headbourne Hybrids' strain, still

Primrose Warburg at home on Boar's Hill near Oxford. A great expert on snowdrops and other bulbs, she had a yellow snowdrop named after her. *Opposite* Not all Valerie's photographs were of rare plants – this is *Bellis perennis*, the common daisy.

Mrs C. Saunders of the Alpine Garden Society and
Lewis 'Luly' Palmer, dressed for cold weather and
admiring an abundance of *Cyclamen libanoticum* at
Palmer's garden at Headbourne Worthy, in Hampshire.

Opposite Dodecatheon 'Red Wings', an American
cowslip from western North America; the original
Iris 'Katharine Hodgkin', bred by E. B. Anderson
and named for the wife of Eliot Hodgkin; *Cyclamen
hederifolium*, the ivy-leaved cyclamen.

popular today. Lewis Palmer, known as 'Luly', was one of those public-spirited gentlemen (in the E. A. Bowles, Dick Trotter and Eliot Hodgkin tradition) who did much unpaid, selfless work for the RHS, including taking on the task of Treasurer between 1953 and 1965. Sir George Taylor, one-time Director of the Royal Botanic Gardens, Kew, called him 'the most knowledgeable botanical horticulturist whose friendship I can claim'. He was also, plainly, a charming man with an excellent sense of humour, kind, modest and scholarly.

As versed in botanical scholarship, although more interested in trees and shrubs perhaps, was Captain Collingwood Ingram, always known to his friends as 'Cherry' because of his pioneering work in introducing Japanese cherries into Britain. Indeed, we all owe him a debt of gratitude for rescuing 'Tai Haku', the Great White Cherry, from possible extinction. He was an avid amateur plant hunter and collector, whose 'Garden of Memories' at Benenden in Kent was crammed with good plants collected on his travels.

One feature of many of these gardeners is how long-lived they were – the beneficial effects of gardening or just plain coincidence, it is hard to say! 'Cherry' Ingram lived to be 100 years old. David Scott, Mary McMurtrie and Joyce Heathcoat Amory are other notable examples. Norman Hadden was a mere 83 when he died in 1971 at 'Underway' in Porlock, Somerset, where he had lived

since 1915. He was particularly interested in woodland plants,
many of which thrived in the temperate conditions of the
Somerset coast. His name is remembered in a dogwood, *Cornus*
'Norman Hadden', one of the finest hybrids ever raised, with
green flowers surrounded by showy creamy-white bracts in early
summer. He had a prodigious knowledge and memory, and his
garden was described as 'a jungle of gems', including alpines,
which surely would have appealed to both Valerie and David.
Generous with his plants, he was a gentle and unassuming man.

Close by, at Bales Mead, was a friend of his, E(dward).
B(ertram). Anderson, until he moved in 1960 to the Old
School House, Little Slaughter, in Gloucestershire. He lived
in a number of other places too, hence the title of his gardening
autobiography, *Seven Gardens or Sixty Years of Gardening*.

Opposite The pristine blossom of an unknown
ornamental cherry (*Prunus*); Captain Collingwood
'Cherry' Ingram (*right*) was a plant explorer and
gardener who did much to popularize Japanese
cherries in English gardens. *Above* Amy (Mrs E. D.)
Doncaster in her garden at Chandlers Ford,
Hampshire, in front of a *Magnolia stellata*. She was
the wife of a great rock gardener and one of the
founder members of the Alpine Garden Society.

A research chemist by profession, he was always a keen grower
of alpines, helping to found the Alpine Garden Society, and
serving as its President in 1948–53. Patrick Synge wrote of his
gardens as '… almost places of pilgrimage for many people …
to see plants that they would find nowhere else.' In his retirement
he became a prolific author of readable gardening books.

Among all this illustrious company, surely the most influential
plantsman of the time, and another friend of Valerie's, was Sir
Eric Savill, who from 1932 developed the so-called Bog Garden in
Windsor Great Park into one of the world's finest woodland
gardens. It ran to 35 acres in extent and was re-named The Savill
Garden, by order of King George VI, in 1951. As well as woodland
plants and wonderful spring bulbs, including an 'alpine meadow'
of 'hoop petticoat' narcissi (*Narcissus bulbocodium*), he also
made a rose garden, an herbaceous border and built a temperate
glasshouse. With Hope Findlay, who became Keeper of the
Gardens in Windsor Great Park in 1943, he laid out the Valley

Opposite Sir Eric Savill in the garden named after him by King George V. Valerie would
often stop by at the garden (*above left*) on her way from Waterperry to Reigate to visit
her parents. *Above right* Hope Findlay worked with Sir Eric, particularly on laying out
the Valley Gardens, and created the Kurume Punch Bowl in Windsor Great Park.

Above Richard (Dick) Trotter at Brin, Inverness-shire,
his home in retirement, with a fine display of
Himalayan blue poppies (*Meconopsis*), which grow
particularly well in the soft Scottish air and peaty soil.
Opposite Meconopsis grandis and *Tulipa sprengeri*, a
species tulip of a particularly lustrous red, which
flourished in The Dower House garden.

Gardens on undulating ground on the northern shore of Virginia Water, close by. It is purposely different from The Savill Garden and contains the famous Punchbowl, where masses of colour-themed Kurume azaleas (sent originally to John Barr Stevenson at nearby Ascot from Japan by Wada the nurseryman) flower in unison in May.

Large public gardens such as The Savill Garden, as well as the botanic gardens at Kew, Edinburgh and Glasnevin, relied partly, of course, on the acquisitions of plant hunters and collectors. The great days of the plant-hunting expeditions were over by then, but there were some people, George Sherriff and Frank Ludlow among them, who continued the time-honoured tradition of the professional, or semi-professional, collector, sponsored by botanical gardens, the Royal Horticultural Society and private gardeners alike to make extended trips in remote regions. Patrick Synge was another plant hunter, whose first expedition in 1932 was to Sarawak, followed by East Africa; in 1960 he set out collecting again, with Paul Furse, this time to Turkey and western Asia. 'Cherry' Ingram, too, was most intrepid, travelling widely in South America, for example, but he was a gentleman amateur who funded his own travels.

'The nicest man I ever knew', was how Valerie
described George Sherriff, seen above and opposite
in the garden at Ascreavie in Scotland which he
developed with his wife, Betty. It featured the
Himalayan vegetation he had seen when acting as
Vice-Consul in Kashgar, and on his plant-collecting
expeditions with Frank Ludlow.

George Sherriff and Frank Ludlow had met in 1928 when
the former was British Vice-Consul and the latter a teacher,
in Kashgar, Tibet. They teamed up to collect plants for British
botanical institutions, such as the Royal Botanic Gardens,
Edinburgh, altogether making seven expeditions in the
Himalaya. Some of these expeditions were at least in part
funded by the RHS, especially those in 1933 and 1936 that yielded
Primula ludlowii and *Primula sherriffae*, *Meconopsis sherriffii* and
Rhododendron sherriffii. Sherriff and his wife, Betty, later created
a garden at Ascreavie in Angus, growing many of the plants that
he had brought back from the Far East. Valerie called him 'the
nicest man I ever knew'.

Ludlow and Sherriff were famous for rhododendrons and
Himalayan poppies (*Meconopsis*); Admiral Paul Furse, on the
other hand, was a bulb man through and through, who went
on a number of expeditions to remote parts of Turkey, Persia
and Afghanistan looking for fritillaries, irises and other flowering
bulbs. He received at least some funding from the Alpine Garden

Society, which was very active in promoting expeditions to mountain places (and indeed still is, although plants are more likely to be photographed than collected these days). Valerie was a great supporter of the Alpine Garden Society, frequently giving illustrated talks to its regional branches. Much younger than the Royal Horticultural Society – founded in 1929 – it nevertheless has become one of the most successful specialist plant societies, with regional and national shows, plant competitions, a first-class journal, a seed exchange and the provision of expert advice.

Another of Valerie's interests in her younger days was painting abstract pictures, which visitors to Boughton were invited to compare to the work of Sam Francis. (She fooled more than one art expert!) And, in addition to all the plantsmen she knew, she also had a number of artist friends and acquaintances – though

Opposite R. B. Cooke, aged 94, in his garden, Kilbryde, Northumberland; and E. R. Dodds, a Professor of Greek at Oxford University and a keen gardener, digging up *Anemone blanda* in Greece. *Above* Greek and Turkish orchids (*left*), and Professor Dodds and Anthony Chevenix-Trench (*right*) in front of a *Cercis* tree in full flower in Greece.

usually they, too, had horticultural or botanical leanings. Among
them were Joan Hassall, the artist and wood-engraver, as well
as Haro Hodson, the cartoonist and mad-keen pug-dog-fancier.
In Scotland, Valerie met Mary McMurtrie, the Scottish
watercolourist and nurserywoman – a remarkable individual
who published her first full-length book, *The Wild Flowers
of Scotland* in 1982, when she was already 80 (she lived to 101).
She lived in Aberdeenshire, where she ran a nursery selling alpines
and other perennials. By all accounts she was a delightful person.

Wilfrid Blunt, another artist photographed by Valerie, was
curator at the Watts Gallery, in Compton, Surrey, for many years.
Formerly an art teacher, he was the author of the pioneering
book *The Art of Botanical Illustration*, with the assistance of
W. T. Stearn. Sir Cedric Morris, a significant twentieth-century
British artist, is known to gardeners as a breeder of bearded irises,

Opposite Mary McMurtrie (*left*), an accomplished watercolourist and nurserywoman, at Balbithan House in Aberdeenshire, and Joan Hassall (*right*), the wood-engraver, sketching in the grounds of Boughton House. *Above* Oncocyclus irises originate from Persia (Iran): these are the most difficult irises to grow in the British climate, and the most sombrely beautiful.

Sir Cedric Morris, the artist, in his garden at Benton
End in Suffolk. Here he bred bearded irises (many
with the word Benton in their names) and selected
cornfield poppies to create his 'Mother of Pearl'
strain. *Opposite* The traditional blood-red cornfield
poppy (*Papaver rhoeas*).

all of which have the prefix 'Benton', named after his house and garden at Benton End in Suffolk. Equally important was his selection of annual poppies, known as 'Mother of Pearl'. Morris would scour the Suffolk countryside looking for cornfield poppies which were not scarlet – the result was an exquisite selection of soft colours, from raspberry-pink to blue-grey and pale purple.

One of Valerie's closest plantsman friends was undoubtedly David Shackleton, whose garden was at Beech Park, Clonsilla, near Dublin. He was born in the house and from 1955 made the traditional walled 1-acre kitchen garden into a plantsman's treasurehouse, or treasuregarden, where herbaceous borders replaced vegetables. Most interested in hardy perennials and alpines, he grew an amazing 34 different species of the New Zealand mountain daisy (*Celmisia*), and Helen Dillon said of him that he was 'perhaps the greatest Irish plantsman of the twentieth century'. In *In an Irish Garden*, by Sybil Connolly and Helen Dillon, David was fulsome in his praise of Valerie: 'The person who contributed most to my interest in alpine plants was Valerie Finnis. … She introduced me to many good nurseries and private gardens, and to her no door was closed. She is probably the most talented plantswoman and propagator I have had the privilege to meet.'

In the same passage, Shackleton also paid tribute to Lord Talbot de Malahide, whom Valerie photographed amongst his Himalayan poppies at Malahide Castle outside Dublin. He had a large estate in Tasmania as well, and travelled widely in the southern hemisphere

Opposite, top to bottom *Galanthus nivalis* (the common –
but exquisite – snowdrop); snowdrops and hellebores; and
a posy made and photographed by Valerie containing 15
different varieties of snowdrop. *Above* Mr and Mrs Gerard
Parker, snowdrop enthusiasts and stalwarts of the Alpine
Garden Society.

after retirement from the Diplomatic Service. Indeed, after a fire
destroyed an area of Tasmania where rare plants grew, he was
able to re-introduce them from his garden at Malahide. He
was part of a circle which also included Lady (Phylis) Moore,
widow of the Keeper of the Glasnevin Botanic Garden in
Dublin. She and her late husband had a 3-acre garden at
Willbrook House, Rathfarnham, near Dublin. She was a
great grower of perennials, silver-leaved plants, old roses and
snowdrops; Graham Thomas wrote of her, and I think it comes
out in Valerie's photographs: '…keen, kindly, and with a good
sense of humour. She had a great influence on Irish horticulture,
and I bless her memory'. All these people Valerie met when she
lectured and travelled in Ireland.

I cannot end without mentioning Wilhelm Schacht, the
Curator of the Munich Botanical Garden, whose influence

Opposite Paeonia 'Phylis Moore' and Phylis,
Lady Moore in person, with her sister. Lady Moore
(*above* making notes in her garden) was the wife of
the Keeper of the National Botanic Gardens, Dublin,
Sir Frederick Moore. After his retirement in 1922,
they moved to Willbrook House, where this picture
was taken.

on Valerie was hugely beneficial. In 1955, aged 31, she was
seriously unwell and had to undergo an operation; to convalesce,
she travelled to the Dolomites with a friend and was given
a letter of introduction to Schacht by Walter Ingwersen, the
famous alpine nurseryman. She stayed for several days and he
taught her about plant photography. 'Not only,' she recalled to
Nigel Colborn, 'did he know more about plants than anybody
else in the world, he is still the finest photographer'. Schacht
gave her one of his Rolleiflexes and inspired her with his
collection of slides of plants growing in their native habitats.
Valerie also visited the Munich Botanical Garden's satellite

Another of Valerie's Irish connections, and one of her closest plantsman friends, was David
Shackleton, here (on the right) with E. B. Anderson in the latter's garden at Bales Mead,
Porlock. Shackleton's garden at Beech Park, near Dublin, was filled with rarities, especially
alpines. *Opposite* Of Lord Talbot de Malahide Valerie noted: 'His castle and gardens were
beautifully kept. He was very careful about naming his plants' – evident in her picture of him.

Norah Warre had a garden in the south of France at the
Villa Roquebrune, near Menton, where Valerie and her
mother Constance spent several summer holidays.
Opposite Eritrichium nanum, the so-called 'King of the
Alps', which only grows in rock above 7,000 feet. This
one was captured by Valerie in the Dolomites, as was her
picture of Wilhelm Schacht, her friend and mentor. In
1955 he gave her a Rolleiflex camera and set her on her way.

garden, the Schachen Alpine Garden, high up in the Wetterstein mountains, next to a hunting lodge of King Ludwig II's.

Generosity plainly characterized Wilhelm Schacht, as it did so many of the other subjects of Valerie's photographs, and indeed Valerie herself. They were very open-handed in giving away plants, often extremely rare ones, to fellow enthusiasts whom they trusted to look after them. The rationale behind this was usually explained by them as self-interested, on the grounds that if they lost their plant they knew where they would be able to go to get one back again, but I think it is much more likely just an overflowing enthusiasm, a desire that others should enjoy the same things that they did. In that respect, gardening and plant-rearing had, and has, a civilizing effect on people or, perhaps more truthfully, appeals strongly to civilized people.

Anna Griffith, in front of her alpine house in her
garden in Cambridge, with a fine display of dwarf
conifers. She was the author of the *Collins Guide
to Alpines and Garden Plants*, which was illustrated
throughout with Valerie's photographs. *Opposite
Primula kewensis* and *Shortia uniflora*. The latter
is an alpine which likes an acid soil in woodland.

Valerie was a plantswoman, first and foremost. Her time
at Waterperry was entirely concerned with the growing of alpine
plants for their individual beauty and interest. Many of her
friends were plantsmen, and she married one. David wrote
about his garden at Boughton in the RHS *Journal* in 1976,
saying that it was not a garden 'but rather a collection of trees
and shrubs and plants. Any vistas or colour effects are purely
accidental. There was never a pre-ordained design. Over the
years I just put in things according to the space available
wherever I thought they would be happiest and look best.
For me the final effect is pleasing, but then I am a plantsman
and ordinary gardeners visiting the garden may be disappointed.'
I don't believe they ever were, for the effect was lovely, with
winding paths through groves of mature trees and shrubs,
and something interesting and unusual at every turn.

Valerie also wrote an article in the *Journal* (the only full-length
one she ever attempted, it seems), in 1973, about moving several

thousand alpine plants to Boughton in a hurry in the June of the
year after her marriage, when the school at Waterperry closed.
(The plants were carefully transported by Pink and Jones, the
Kettering removal firm, and she expressed her delight to them that
the worms that came with them had travelled well in the van and
were safely established at Boughton.) She explained how the
solution to housing her plants had been to erect raised beds, made
of second-hand railway sleepers, along the north and south walls
of the vegetable garden, which was situated just below David's
shrub garden, as well as in the Hawk Yard adjacent to it. She also
brought with her a collection of 22 stone troughs, filled with
'treasures'. Growing alpines in troughs was an idea popularized by
Clarence Elliott, owner of the Six Hills Nursery in Stevenage;
indeed, he may well have given some of the troughs to Valerie.

  'A visitor to these raised beds will find no exciting colour
schemes. I have said that I planted madly at the start and so
I did. I had to! Apart from seeing that quick spreaders were not
planted up against dwarfs I just put in the plants as they came to
hand, so to speak. I don't believe that alpine plants can ever clash
and if occasionally I produce something that looks like a carefully

Opposite left Valerie grew many of her 'treasures'
in stone troughs – she brought 22 of them to
Boughton (along with some worms) when the
school at Waterperry closed; *opposite right* one
of David's plant selections was this mallow, *Malva*
'Brave Heart'. *Above* David weeding among
Valerie's alpines, in his customary gardening gear.

planned group it is entirely by accident.' This article says a great deal about Valerie: she wrote, as she spoke, in an unconstrained, spontaneous way; and it is full of good sense and deep, practical knowledge. It accords perfectly with David's view as well. She went on: 'Like most plantsmen I am an incurable magpie, and I cannot resist acquiring and trying to grow in the open a lot of plants which need alpine house conditions. My little alpine house is over full and anyhow I much prefer plants in the open ground rather than in pots.' And since many growers consider Kabschia and Engleria saxifrages as subjects for the alpine house, it shows what a fine gardener she was.

From time to time, for twenty years or so from the mid-1950s, Valerie would send a short 'Note from a Fellow' to the *Journal*, accompanied by one of her photographs, concerning a plant which she had raised at Waterperry, or seen in a garden or nursery she had visited. Always interesting and to the point, these helped establish Valerie, in the eyes of knowledgeable gardeners, as both rock plant expert and highly talented garden photographer, even if the quality of the picture reproduction in those days left something to be desired. Or so we would think now.

Of course, Valerie's treasures needed constant attention and, in later years, when she became

David sitting in the sun, towered over by the Scotch thistle, *Onopordum acanthium*, in Valerie's garden.

frail and bent, a number were lost. But, in her photographs, it
can be seen how they looked in the heyday of The Dower House
garden. They were a remarkable and thrilling sight, on a sunny
morning in late spring, any time in the 1970s. And that is how
I like to remember the garden and its makers: David carefully
hand-weeding amongst the rock plants in the raised beds,
kneelers strapped on, soft canvas shoes on his feet, and a battered
brown trilby on his head. While, close by, in the Hawk Yard,
Valerie calls out from the shed where she is potting up seedlings,
and blackbirds sing from the top of the kitchen garden wall,
against which grows a morello cherry, covered thick as snow in
white blossom.

Opposite Gillenia trifoliata, a native of North American woodlands, at The Dower House
– a plant of great importance to David and Valerie since it was the means of introducing them
to each other in 1968 at Waterperry. *Above* David and Valerie, with their pug Kate, sitting
outside The Dower House, where they lived and gardened together in great harmony.

VALERIE FINNIS: GARDENER AND PHOTOGRAPHER

Anna Pavord

For almost 30 years, Valerie Finnis was a distinguished and charismatic teacher at the Waterperry Horticultural School for Women, near Oxford, founded in 1932 by the fearsomely smocked and gaitered Beatrix Havergal. Miss Havergal believed in the wholesome benefits of practical labour and Finnis, who arrived there as a student in 1942 – she was just 18 years old – had vivid recollections of the 25-acre field into which she was pitched with two Land Girls. Learning to drive the Ferguson tractor was her first great triumph. She said it was one of the first models that Ferguson ever made.

She learnt how to drive a lorry there, too, to get their home-grown blackcurrants and potatoes to the covered market in Oxford and crates of Waterperry apples and pears up to Covent Garden market in London. That meant starting out at half past three in the morning. No hardship, she said. The dormitories at Waterperry were colder than ice.

Alpine plants became her great speciality and when, after the Second World War, Finnis decided to stay on as a teacher at Waterperry, she set up a nursery there, selling the difficult saxifrages and miffy drabas that alpine gardeners so adore. Rockeries had been a rage in the Thirties and Finnis built up a great reputation for her nursery; she became one of the most skilful propagators of demanding plants in England.

In the early Fifties she acquired her first camera, an old Rolleiflex given to her by Wilhelm Schacht, curator of the Munich Botanical Garden, who shared her passion for alpine plants. She used the same camera for 40 years, one of the first women to specialize in photographing plants and gardens. She captured many of the gardening icons of that post-war age: Rhoda, Lady Birley (mother of Mark Birley of Annabel's) rakishly

Opposite Valerie, in a photograph taken by Howard Sooley in 2006.

wound in scarves while tending the borders at Charleston, Vita Sackville-West glaring from an archway at Sissinghurst, the painter Cedric Morris among his irises at Benton End in Suffolk, Nancy Lancaster in a stylish cuffed Fifties jacket watering her flowers at Haseley Court in Oxfordshire. Finnis never took more than one exposure of each subject. Film was too expensive to waste.

Her life – travelling, lecturing, taking photographs, tending the alpine plants in her nursery – changed radically in 1970 when she married Sir David Scott, a cousin of the 8th Duke of Buccleuch. After retiring from the Foreign Office, Scott had spent 40 years building up a fine garden of trees and shrubs at The Dower House of Boughton House in Northamptonshire. She often described their first meeting:

> I was in my awful old dungarees in the potting shed at Waterperry and a voice outside said, 'She's got *Gillenia trifoliata.*' I came out and replied, 'You're the first person who's ever known that plant.' That was David. We just sort of fitted in.

Her fine collection of alpines went with her to The Dower House, planted out in troughs and paving in the enclosed courtyard by the front door. For the next 16 years the Scotts worked together in the garden, digging, scything, propagating, tying in climbers. She was 46 when she married, he 82, but they never thought of age, she said.

Alongside the Waterperry Finnis (the girls always called each other by their surnames), the dungarees and digging side, there existed a completely different Finnis, actressy, mischievous, a woman who adored gossip and outrageous hats. She joined the exclusive circle of People who kept Pugs, the last of her pug dogs a beguiling barrel-shaped creature called Sophie. She knew most of the people who mattered in the gardening world and many of them were invited to The Dower House, where they would usually be photographed and asked to write in one of her extraordinary scrap-books.

She had a knack for engineering spectacular fallings-out with people, a process she thoroughly enjoyed. She was a great chronicler of her age and a terrific letter-writer. I've kept every one she sent me. Her handsome, determined script circles round and round the edges of the writing paper, as new, often surreal thoughts exploded from what she had originally written on the page.

For years, she served on various prestigious plant committees of the Royal Horticultural Society and in 1975 was awarded their ultimate accolade, the Victoria Medal of Honour. Several fine plants commemorate her expertise: *Viola* 'Boughton Blue', *Hebe cupressoides* 'Boughton Dome', *Muscari* 'Valerie Finnis'. She was an extremely effective ally in the fracas in 1995 that surrounded the RHS's plans to move their world-class library out of London. That was when she acquired her nickname 'Mole', a role she adored and in which she was astonishingly effective.

She was always generous to people starting off in the plant business. Carol Klein of Glebe Cottage Plants (now a television presenter on *Gardeners' World*) remembers the first time she showed at the RHS in London, a daunting occasion. 'Finnis adored the plants. She noticed things that other people missed.' When at the Chelsea Flower Show, Klein was disappointed to get only a silver medal for a show garden, Finnis came to the stand with a banana inscribed 'Gold Medal awarded to Glebe Cottage Plants by Valerie Finnis'.

Finnis had no children of her own but in 1990 set up The Merlin Trust in memory of her husband and his only son, Merlin, who was killed in North Africa in May 1941. The trust gives grants to young gardeners and plantsmen who need money for particular projects or travel associated with their studies. 'I love helping the young to get on,' she used to say. 'For years plants used to be more important than people to me. But really it's only people that matter.'

GARDEN LIVES

Brent Elliott

David Scott scything in the garden at The Dower House.
Page 137 A cyclamen and a primula.
Pages 138–39 (top, left to right) Agapanthus, hellebore, ranunculus, *Gentiana farreri; (centre, left to right)* dahlia, *Inula orientalis, Allium cristophii, Eranthis hyemalis; (bottom, left to right)* rose, *Anemone blanda* 'White Splendour', *Tulipa kaufmanniana, Kniphofia* 'Prince Igor'.

Numbers in **bold** after each entry refer to pages where text or illustrations relating to the subject appear.

Amory, Sir John Heathcoat, 3rd Baronet

Born 2 May 1894, died 22 November 1972
VMH 1966

Amory, Joyce, Lady

Born 17 November 1901, died 18 November 1981

Sir John Heathcoat Amory inherited the Knightshayes estate in Devon after the death of his father in 1931. In 1937, he married Joyce Wethered, a prize-winning golfer. Their horticultural activities at Knightshayes did not really begin until after the War, when they began developing the surrounding woodland, and expanded the garden to 12 acres. The original garden had been laid out by Edward Kemp in the 1890s; new formal gardens were now added, a famous topiary foxhunt was cut along the top of a hedge, and peat walls were erected to house a collection of ericaceous plants. Plants such as *Anemone nemorosa* 'Knightshayes Vestal' and *Betula utilis* 'Knightshayes' show the directions in which their planting was taking them. Lady Amory, the more innovative horticulturist, became a member of the RHS Picture and Floral B Committees.

In his later years Sir John increasingly relied on an electric chair, but was notorious for leaving it behind when showing visitors around. 'As a result', Patrick Synge recorded, 'often there would be heard, echoing round the garden, the plaintive cry "Where did I leave my something chair?"' After his death the garden was acquired by the National Trust. **78–80, 103**

Anderson, Edward Bertram

Born 23 August 1885, died 29 July 1971
VMH 1960; Cory Cup 1969; Lyttel Cup 1971

E. B. Anderson was a research chemist for United Dairies, but his reputation rested on his skill and knowledge in growing alpines, for which he became known in the years after the First World War. A founder member of the Alpine Garden Society, he served as its President in 1948–53, and also presided over the Second International Rock Garden Conference (1951). He bred a large number of alpine bulbs, among them irises such as 'Mary Barnard', and most famous of all, 'Katharine Hodgkin', named after the wife of his friend Eliot Hodgkin, for which he was awarded the Cory Cup for best new cultivar in 1969.

His most famous gardens he developed late in life: first Bales Mead, at Porlock in Somerset, where he moved to in 1950; and, after his wife's death, the Old School House, Lower Slaughter, near Cheltenham. In his 60s, Anderson became a prolific author. In 1959, he wrote a book on *Rock Gardens* for a popular series published by Penguin, in association with the RHS, and five years later followed it with *Hardy Bulbs*, volume 1. He also wrote *Dwarf Bulbs for the Rock Garden* (1959); *Camellias* (1961); *The Oxford Book of Wild Flowers* (1963); *Gardening on Chalk and Limestone* (1965); *The Small Rock Garden* (1965); and his autobiography, *Seven Gardens* (1973), which was seen through the press after his death by Eliot Hodgkin and Patrick Synge.

In July 1971 he went on an expedition to the Dolomites, and was said by fellow travellers to be 'as agile as a goat', but on return he suffered a series of heart attacks. He lived long enough to learn that he had been awarded the Lyttel Cup for his work on lilies. **56, 57, 102, 104, 107, 121, 122**

Annesley, Richard Grove

Born 1879, died 1966

Grove Annesley was famous as the proprietor of Annes Grove in County Cork, which he inherited in 1900. Annesley was a cousin of the Earl of Annesley who developed the arboretum at Castlewellan, and a lifelong friend of the 4th Lord Headfort, who introduced him to

From the top: The Heathcoat Amorys; E. B. Anderson; Rhoda, Lady Birley, and in her office with her secretary; Wilfrid Blunt at the Watts Gallery, Compton.

George Forrest. Annesley became one of Forrest's sponsors, and also helped to fund expeditions by Frank Kingdon-Ward, receiving quantities of new rhododendrons and other plants. He developed a rock garden by clearing existing trees and exposing the stones beneath, and created a water garden with waterlilies and Robinsonian wild planting along its banks. Within the walled garden he laid out a series of compartments containing borders devoted to groups of single plant genera. Annes Grove became one of the most famous gardens in Ireland, and after Annesley's death continued to be maintained by his son. 84, 87

Aslet, Wilfred Kenneth
Born 4 October 1908, died 10 August 1980
AOH 1968
Ken Aslet began working for his father, a gardener, before he was 10. Successively apprenticed to the nurseries of Carliles, William Wood and Toynbees, where he worked his way up to become Nursery Manager, he moved to Wisley in 1949, as Rock Garden Foreman. By the time he succeeded to the role of Superintendent of the Rock Garden in 1961, he had already become identified with the Wisley rock garden in the public's eyes.

In his spare time Aslet served as Chairman of the East Surrey Group of the Alpine Garden Society, and took tours to the Alps and Middle East. His duties for the RHS included making rock gardens for show purposes: he organized rock gardens for two International Rock Garden Plant Conferences, in 1961 and 1971, and in 1968 he supervised the creation of a rock garden for the Chelsea Flower Show, to fill the gap when not a single commercial firm had put in a proposal for a rock garden on the traditional Rock Garden Bank site. Aslet retired from Wisley in 1975. 19, 54, 55

Birley, Rhoda
Born 1900, died 15 June 1981
Rhoda Vava Mary Lecky Pike was born into the Anglo-Irish Ascendancy, the daughter of Robert Lecky Pike of Kilnock, Thurlow. Already a highly regarded beauty in her teens, in 1921 she married the society painter Oswald Birley, 20 years her senior. His studio on Wellington Road, St John's Wood, was the centre for their social life, focused on the art world and the ballet.

Around 1930, the Birleys bought Charleston Manor in Sussex, and embarked on a programme of restoration and development. Walter Godfrey was hired to remodel the house and turn the barn into a concert hall. Lady Birley tackled the gardens, with a basic design by Godfrey and an indeterminate degree of advice from such friends as Gertrude Jekyll and Vita Sackville-West; Harold Hillier advised on tree planting in the later stages of work. Beginning in 1935, the Birleys convened a summer festival of music, dance and talks on gardening. After Sir Oswald's death in 1952, Lady Birley continued the festivals into the 1970s, despite increasing ill health; the custom was revived in 1986, and continues still. 61, 82–83, 135

Blunt, Wilfrid Jasper Walter
Born 19 July 1901, died 8 January 1987
VMM 1951
Wilfrid Blunt was the son of the vicar of St John's, Paddington, and the elder brother of the art historian and spy Anthony Blunt (of whose treason he said that he had been completely ignorant). He spent much of his career as an art teacher, first at Haileybury (1923–38) and then at Eton (1938–59). In 1959 he became the Curator of the Watts Gallery in Compton, near Guildford, a post which he occupied for the rest of his life. He published books on many subjects: a biography of G.F. Watts, poetry and fiction, travel – and, eventually, horticultural history.

In 1950 he published his two pioneering books: *Tulipomania*, and, assisted by W. T. Stearn, *The Art of Botanical Illustration*. This book, the first important history of its subject, earned him the Veitch Memorial Medal from the RHS. He went on to collaborate with Sacheverell Sitwell and Patrick Synge on *Great Flower Books* (1956), and with Sandra Raphael on *The Illustrated Herbal* (1979). On other botanical subjects, his most important works were his biography of Linnaeus, *The Compleat Naturalist* (1971), and his history of Kew Gardens, *In for a Penny* (1978 – the following year the entrance fee was increased for the first time in a century). He was also an enthusiastic grower of poppies, and contributed a series of articles on *Papaveraceae* to the RHS Journal, *The Garden*, in the 1980s. 114

Boothman, Stuart
Born 26 January 1906, died 10 February 1976
Stuart Boothman began his career as a bank clerk, but on coming into an inheritance, abandoned the bank and moved into horticulture. Like his Scottish rival Jack Drake, he studied under Walter Ingwersen, and in 1933 set up his own Nightingale Nursery at Furze Platt, near Maidenhead. He was one of the founders of the Alpine Garden Society, and its Hon. Show Secretary for its first three years; after the War he served as the Secretary of the Berkshire branch. His only book was *The Alpine House and its Plants* (1938).

'He was a rebel and very decidedly anti-establishment', Kath Dryden remembered. On her first visit to his nursery, he accosted her as she wandered around with her nearly empty basket and asked if she was hard up. When she replied that she didn't know what to choose, he filled her basket with plants for free and told her, 'Come back when you've killed that lot'.

Boothman's wife died in 1968, and the following year's catalogue contained the announcement that it would be his last. In 1970 he sold the nursery and moved to Wales for his final years. 50, 51

Bowes Lyon, Sir David
Born 2 May 1902, died 13 September 1961
VMH 1953
Sir David Bowes Lyon was the younger brother of Elizabeth, the Queen Mother, with whom he shared a common interest in gardening; but in his case it was to take

a professional turn. When told by his
doctors that he needed an open-air
occupation, he went to Kew as a student
gardener for a year, under the tutelage of
Frank Knight, later Director of Wisley.

Having joined the Council of the
RHS in 1934, he served as the Society's
Treasurer from 1948 to 1953, and then,
on the death of the second Baron
Aberconway, succeeded him as President.
While in office, he helped to found the
British Committee for Overseas Flower
Shows, and was involved with British
exhibits at the Ghent Floralies; he
presided over lily and orchid conferences;
he chaired the Joint Gardens Committee
of the RHS and the National Trust.
He died suddenly in 1961, and was
succeeded as President by the third
Baron Aberconway. Bowes Lyon was
Lord Lieutenant of Hertfordshire, and
lived at St Paul's Walden Bury, where
he restored the structure of an early
18th-century garden: 'the garden not only
of an artist but of a first-class plantsman'. **55**

Campbell, May Sherwood

Born 9 March 1903, died 11 August 1982
Maybud Campbell was so called to
distinguish her from her mother, also
May. She was born in Streatham, London,
but grew up partly at Layer Marney
Tower, Essex. She had a brief career
as a concert singer at the Wigmore Hall.

She joined the Wild Flower Society
and the Botanical Exchange Club in the
1920s, and in 1932 became one of the first
local secretaries (for Essex) for the latter.
Her career with the Club saw a hiatus
in 1938, when she resigned after an
argument with P. M. Hall over a paper
on *Dactylorrhiza* which she regarded as
insulting to her friend A. J. Willmott;
but after Hall's death she rejoined, and in
1947 became the General Secretary,
presiding over the Club's transformation
into the Botanical Society of the British
Isles. For many years she made an annual

Maybud Campbell

botanical foray to the Outer Hebrides,
and in 1945 published a *Flora of Uig*.

After 1950 she took over the villa Val
Rahmeh at Menton, where her father had
lived; she grew citrus fruits, and once
staged an exhibit of them at the Chelsea
Flower Show. In the 1960s she acquired a
second villa, at Chernex in the Swiss Alps,
which she named Casa Rossa. She sold
Val Rahmeh to the Jardin des Plantes, but
kept a pavilion there until 1980. Forced
out of Switzerland, she moved to a flat
near Grasse, and lastly to Roquebrune at
Cap Martin, where she died.   **85, 86, 87**

Codrington, John

Born 28 October 1898, died 25 April 1991
VMM **1988; Greek Military Cross**
John Codrington followed his father and
grandfather into the Coldstream Guards,
and saw action on the Western Front in
1917. His military and diplomatic career
was varied, secretive and occasionally
controversial: liaison work with the Greek
army during the Turkish war; Military
Intelligence in the Second World War,
posing as a government official in
Gibraltar while helping Allied prisoners
of war to escape; then liaison work with
French intelligence services in London,
when he was exposed in the press for
holding down a second job as a drayman
between assignments. After the War, he
worked as an adviser to the filmmaker
Alexander Korda, then for BOAC.

Meanwhile, he had begun gardening,
'worshipping at the shrine of Clarence
Elliott', and designing gardens. He had
already made alterations to the garden at
Rockingham Castle as a teenager, and on
retiring in 1960, he turned to garden
design as a second career. He made or
altered gardens in Britain, Europe,
Australia, India, Africa and Papua New
Guinea; when a group of subalterns
claimed to be the first Coldstream Guards
to visit Timbuktu, he pointed out that he
had preceded them (and in fact they had
been photographed standing in a garden
he had made). He himself had two small
gardens: Ranelagh Cottage in Pimlico,
and Stone Cottage, Hambleton. The latter
garden was left to him in 1960 by his
sister. In an article in *The Garden*, he said
of it: 'My garden is not a normal, civilized
garden. It is a mad, wild jungle…. full of
weeds, which I call wild flowers'. **76–78**

Cooke, Randle Blair

**Born 1 September 1890, died 13 October
1973**
VMH **1959**
R. B. Cooke was a timber broker, but
retired early in order to concentrate on
gardening. He helped to sponsor the
expeditions of Reginald Farrer, George
Forrest and Frank Kingdon-Ward; he met
Forrest shortly before his last journey, and
taught him colour photography, of which

R. B. Cooke

Cooke was an amateur pioneer. Kilbryde, his garden in Northumberland, was about an acre (not counting a quarry), on a steep north-facing slope. Here he built up what was described as 'a virtually unrivalled collection of rare and difficult plants which by some subtle alchemy of his own he grew to perfection.' As well as rhododendrons and other ericaceous plants, he grew *Carpenteria californica* in the open air, and built a special 'cave' for *Philesia magellanica*. He bred meconopsis (e.g. *Meconopsis* x *cookei*) and cassiopes, and his name is commemorated in *Rhododendron cookeianum*. Increasingly blind in his later years, he was looked after by his housekeeper Miss Brady. 56, 57, 100, 112

Crook, Herbert Clifford
Born 16 April 1882, died 1 May 1974
Clifford Crook served as Show Secretary to the Alpine Garden Society, and was an early recipient of its Lyttel Trophy. He devoted his life to *Campanulaceae*, on which he published two books: his major monograph, *Campanulas* (1951), and a smaller horticultural book, *Campanulas and Bellflowers in Cultivation* (1959). Kath Dryden recalled that 'Clifford's garden was dominated by the genus *Campanula* and I came away in a lavender-blue haze with nomenclatural indigestion, and a bag of plants.' In his later years his eyesight and hearing both failed (he had once been a pianist), but he maintained an alpine house till the end, and left his massive notes on *Campanulaceae* to the Alpine Garden Society. 100

Dahl, Roald
Born 13 September 1916, died 23 November 1990
Neal, Patricia
Born 20 January 1926
Roald Dahl was born in Cardiff, and saw service as a fighter pilot in the Second

Patricia Neal and Tessa Dahl

World War, achieving the rank of Wing Commander. His first children's book, *The Gremlins*, was published in 1942, and he went on to an extraordinarily successful career as a children's author, writer of stories of suspense and, in the 1980s, presenter of a television series based on his *Tales of the Unexpected*. A garden in his honour was exhibited at the 2006 Chelsea Flower Show.

In 1953 Dahl married the American actress Patricia Neal, who had become famous for her role in the 1949 film of *The Fountainhead*. She later won an Academy Award for Best Actress for her role in *Hud* (1963). In 1965 she suffered an aneurysm, spent three weeks in a coma, and had to relearn to walk and talk under Dahl's supervision. The couple divorced in 1983, and Patricia Neal now lives in America. 80–82

Dodds, Eric Robertson
Born 26 July 1893, died 8 April 1979
E. R. Dodds was born in County Down and educated at Oxford, where he met some of his lifelong friends, such as Aldous Huxley and T. S. Eliot. In 1914 he obtained a first in Classics, but was later expelled for his support of the Easter Rising; he had already seen war service as a medical orderly in Serbia. After the War he lectured in Classics at Reading University, and married Annie Powell, a lecturer in English there. In 1924 he

became Professor of Greek at Birmingham, where the poets W. H. Auden and Louis MacNeice were among his students; in 1936 he was appointed Regius Professor of Greek at Oxford. His major work, *The Greeks and the Irrational* (1951), helped to popularize the distinction between guilt cultures and shame cultures.

Dodds never attracted attention in the horticultural world, but gardening was his major extracurricular interest. MacNeice, in his poem *Autumn Sequel* (1954), introduced him as a character under the name of 'Boyce, both classical scholar and gardener', and said of him:

> there comes a stir / Alike among Greek roots and roots of flowers / When Boyce bends over them. Each blight and blur / And slur and slug and sheer hiatus cowers, / And garbled soil and pest-infested page / Become themselves, thanks to his cleansing powers…

His 'garden with its straight / Borders and close-napped lawns and apple trees', never written up in the gardening magazines, was well known to those in his literary and scholarly circles. 112, 113

Doncaster, Amy
Born 11 April 1894, died 31 December 1995
Amy Baring worked for the famous lily grower Lyttell in his garden at Nyewoods for many years. From 1931, she lived at a house in Chandlers Ford; the garden had oak trees and scrub when she moved in, and she began planting rhododendrons and woodland plants. In 1947 she married E. D. Doncaster, a mountain climber and plant hunter who collected in the Balkans, and who was the Secretary of the Hampshire branch of the Alpine Garden Society. As his wedding present, he gave her an adjoining piece of land into which to expand their garden. The marriage was brief, for he died in 1950. She remained at Chandlers Ford until her death, growing snowdrops, daffodils, hellebores,

epimediums, bergenias and a range of other plants. Her garden developed a great reputation among plantsmen, but was hardly known to the wider world until Roy Lancaster described it in *The Garden* in 1981. She is commemorated by *Geranium sylvaticum* 'Amy Doncaster'. 98, 99, 105

Drake, Jack

Born *c.* 1909, died 4 December 1997
VMH 1978

Jack Drake began as a sugar broker in the family business, but his interest in plants quickly came to the fore. In 1936 he started working with Walter Ingwersen in Sussex; together they collected plants in the Rocky Mountains. In 1938 his father retired and moved to Aviemore, in Inverness-shire; Jack Drake started his own nursery in Aviemore that year. The first year was a disaster, with a heavy loss of plants, but Drake started using the newly introduced John Innes composts, and soon the nursery was prospering. It had to close during the War, but reopened in 1945. The Inshriach Alpine Nursery was one of the most famous alpine nurseries of the second half of the century. With the skilful John Lawson as an assistant from 1949, and a partner from 1955, the nursery produced profitable lines of dianthus, primulas, gentians and phlox. Drake retired in 1971, but the nursery stayed in the family and continues to be a success. 36, 37, 50

Elliott, Clarence

Born 3 November 1881, died 18 February 1969
VMH 1951; VMM 1954; Sander Medal, 1935

Clarence Elliott was only a year younger than Reginald Farrer, whom he was to succeed as the great authority on alpines. He gained experience working for Rivers' nursery at Sawbridgeworth, for Backhouse in York, and travelling in South Africa. In 1910 he accompanied Farrer on a tour of the Alps, which Farrer described in his book *Among the Hills*. He had already founded his own nursery in Stevenage, in 1907.

The Six Hills Nursery was to be one of the most important alpine nurseries of the interwar years. Many eminent alpine growers passed through its doors, among them Frank Barker, later the author of *The Cream of Alpines*, who eventually succeeded him. Elliott himself wrote only one book, *Rock Garden Plants* (1935), but he wrote articles for the *Birmingham Post*, the *Sunday Times* and the *Illustrated London News* – and catalogues. Some of John Nash's first published illustrations were in the 1926 limited-edition Six Hills catalogue, and Nash dedicated his book *Poisonous Plants* to Elliott.

The number of plants that Elliott introduced is enormous, as is the number of plants named after either him or the Six Hills Nursery: from arenarias to verbenas with primulas, geraniums, saxifrages, and osteospermums in between. He collected plants in the Falkland Islands and Chile. But his major significance for rock gardening lay in his promotion of the alpine lawn, his discovery of the virtues of tufa as an environment for saxatile plants, and his popularizing of miniature gardens made in stone troughs – his first exhibit of these was at Chelsea in 1923.

Clarence Elliott

After the Second World War, Stevenage New Town began to encroach on his nursery, and Elliott moved to Broadwell, near his son Joe's alpine nursery, leaving the Six Hills Nursery to Frank Barker.   39, 52, 128

Findlay, Thomas Hope

Born 21 April 1910, died 19 October 1994
VMH 1961; AOH 1957; LVH 1975; Loder Rhododendron Cup 1979; Lyttel Cup 1957; A. J. Waley Medal 1956

Hope Findlay was the son of Robert Findlay, the head gardener at Logan and Castle Kennedy, who moved to London after the First World War to become, first, the Superintendent of Greenwich Park, and then the Keeper of Wisley (1925–38). After training at nearby Pyrford Court, and then at Bodnant, Hope Findlay became head gardener at Heywood Garden near Cobham, at the age of 21. After a succession of other positions, he arrived in 1943 at Windsor Great Park, where he became assistant to Eric Savill.

Findlay assisted Savill on the later works at The Savill Garden, and assumed responsibility for the exhibits the Royal Park mounted at flower shows. He was a skilled plant breeder, and during the 1940s and 1950s he bred a large number of rhododendrons, going successively through pink, red, and yellow phases in his preferred flower colours. But his major work was the planting of the Valley Garden in Windsor Great Park. John Barr Stevenson had built up a major rhododendron collection at Tower Court, Ascot, all planted in the series which formed the accepted classification of species at the time; Findlay oversaw their transplantation to the new garden, and created the Kurume Punch Bowl, a massive arrangement of Kurume azaleas that had been sent to Stevenson by the Japanese nurseryman Wada. Findlay was concerned with colour effects in a way that Savill was not, and the Punch

Bowl became one of the icons of mid-century gardening in Britain. 107, 109

Fish, Margery
Born 5 August 1892, died 25 March 1969
VMH 1963

Margery Townsend began her career as a secretarial assistant on the *Daily Mail*, eventually working her way up to become Lord Northcliffe's secretary. During the First World War, she formed part of Northcliffe's staff on the British mission to the United States, for which she was awarded the MBE. After the war, she went back to work for the *Mail*, as secretary to its editor, Walter Fish, whom she married in 1933. In 1937 they bought East Lambrook Manor in Somerset; in those days she wasn't yet a gardener, and their garden reflected Walter's taste, with borders of brightly coloured dahlias.

Gradually developing a horticultural expertise, and responding both to the need to garden without a large staff, and to the taste for what were called 'cottage garden plants', Fish redeveloped the garden – not without opposition from Walter. She built up a network of enthusiastic plantsmen who exchanged plants and advice, and her garden came to boast large and idiosyncratic collections of silver-leaved plants, daphnes, heucheras, viburnums, euphorbias, carpeting plants and old-fashioned perennials. From the mid-1950s she ran a nursery at East Lambrook Manor. A large number of cultivars, ranging from *Bergenia* 'Margery Fish', through *Santolina* 'Lambrook Silver' and *Crocosmia* 'Lambrook Gold', to *Ranunculus ficaria* 'Lambrook Black', commemorate her or the garden of their origin.

Margery Fish's books have been reissued over and over again, and most are still in print. She began with an account of the creation of her garden at Lambrook Manor, *We Made a Garden* (1956), and proceeded to write a series of practical

Margery Fish

manuals: *An All the Year Garden* (1958); *Cottage Garden Flowers* (1961); *Ground Cover Plants* (1964); *Gardening in the Shade* (1964); *A Flower for Every Day* (1965); *Carefree Gardening* (1966). These works brought her a widespread popularity outside her circle of plant enthusiasts. 59, 60-65, 68

Furse, John Paul Wellington
Born 13 October 1894, died 8 October 1978
OBE 1946; CB 1958; VMH 1965
Lyttel Lily Cup 1968

Paul Furse had a distinguished career in the Royal Navy, serving on submarines during the interwar years, and becoming Assistant Naval Attaché in Europe and the Americas during the Second World War. After the War he held a series of positions and reached the rank of Rear-Admiral before his retirement in 1959.

After retiring, Furse began a second career as a plant collector. In 1960 he travelled through Turkey and Iran with Patrick Synge, and made three further expeditions in western Asia. Synge later referred to him as 'the father figure of all young plant collectors in the Middle East'. Most of the plants he collected were bulbs, and he was particularly interested in irises, crocuses and *Liliaceae*.

He used his own garden to raise much of the seed he brought back, and drew the different forms as they appeared. He had begun exhibiting drawings of flowers at

RHS shows in the 1920s, and later became a member of the Society's Picture Committee. Today his drawings are divided between the Royal Horticultural Society and the Royal Botanic Gardens, Kew. Synge wrote an appreciation of his paintings in the Alpine Garden Society's *Bulletin* for 1977. 109, 112

Griffith, Anna Nellie
Born 10 January 1889, died 1 October 1974

Anna Griffith turned to gardening as a means of coping with bereavement, after the death of her first husband in 1916; and bereavement continued to measure out her life, as her second husband died in 1941, followed by one of her sons; she was injured by an accident in her later years. In 1930, she saw an advertisement for the newly founded Alpine Garden Society, and soon became an active member and official. She made several plant collecting trips to the Alps, carrying with her a quantity of egg boxes in which she placed cuttings; she refused on principle ever to dig up a plant in the wild.

For 40 years she lived at Paradise House, next to a bird sanctuary near Cambridge. Here she wrote her *Collins Guide to Alpines* (1964), illustrated with photographs by Valerie Finnis. In her last years she moved to a small house in Hampshire, where she was starting a new rock garden when she died. 14, 126

Paul Furse and his wife

Hadden, Norman

Born 21 March 1888, died June 1971
VMH 1962

Norman Hadden's family visited Porlock in 1915, and decided to make it their home. Young Norman was an enthusiast for iris species, and in 1923 went plant collecting with W. R. Dykes, the author of *The Genus Iris.* James Platt later described his garden at Underway: 'At a glance the visitor to Underway would say the garden was one of flowering trees and shrubs only. Before long the same visitor would realize that the whole series of small gardens was carpeted with herbs and bulbs, many of them rare and unusual, luxuriating and sowing themselves freely in the fertile soil and mild climate of Porlock.' His name is commemorated in cultivars of *Agapanthus* and *Cornus.*

In addition to bulbs, he was also devoted to butterflies and birds, and to breeding Shetland sheep dogs. For his last 30 years, he was looked after by his housekeeper Mrs Edwards, who stayed on after his death to maintain his garden. 97, 103–04

Hassall, Joan

Born 3 March 1906, died 6 March 1988

Joan Hassall was the daughter of the Skegness artist John Hassall, and the elder sister of the actor and poet Christopher Hassall. Having studied at the Royal Academy Schools, she began her career as an artist by illustrating a volume of her brother's poems; the publishers, Heinemann, at first rejected the idea of using an unknown artist, but the family insisted, and Heinemann became so enthusiastic about her work that they commissioned her to illustrate Francis Brett Young's *Portrait of a Village* (1937). (Late in life, she was the first president of the Francis Brett Young Society.)

Hassall idolized the artist and engraver Thomas Bewick (1753–1828), and took

him as a model for her work as a wood-engraver. She taught at the School of Photo-engraving and Lithography in Fleet Street until the Second World War and spent the war years teaching at the Edinburgh College of Art. After the war, and a brief venture as the director of a private press, the Curtain Press, her work began to attract official favour and recognition. In 1948 she became the first woman to design a British stamp (for the wedding of Princess Elizabeth), and four years later she was invited to engrave the invitation for the new Queen's Coronation. She continued through a long career to promote wood-engraving, and to illustrate books. 114, 115

Havergal, Grace Beatrix Helen

Born 7 July 1901, died 7 April 1980
VMM 1959; VMH 1965

Beatrix Havergal was the daughter of the Vicar of Bressingham in Norfolk. She trained at the Thatcham Fruit and Flower Farm School at Newbury, obtained first class honours on the RHS examinations, and got her first job as a housekeeper and gardener at Downe House School, where she met her lifelong partner Avice Sanders. The two pooled their money to rent a cottage and walled garden at Pusey House, near Faringdon, and start a small-scale horticultural college. In 1932 they rented larger premises from Magdalen College, Oxford: Waterperry House, which was to become the last of the important female horticultural colleges.

In order to teach the students about the marketing of produce as well as its cultivation, Waterperry began to supply fruit and vegetables to regional markets, eventually including London. A series of Gold Medals for displays of strawberries – 15 out of 16 successive years, 1955 to 1970 – at the Chelsea Flower Show cemented their reputation (and that of Joan Stokes, the supervisor of the glasshouse department) and made Waterperry visibly

Beatrix Havergal

familiar to the gardening public. Havergal became a member of the RHS Examinations Board. But the reorganization of education in the 1950s and 1960s brought renewed difficulties for the school; the Pilkington Report opposed the idea of single-sex schools. Havergal tried to have Waterperry declared a county college, and the RHS proposed turning it into a charitable trust, but in 1971 Waterperry finally closed as a college. 10, 14, 25–32, 34, 64, 80, 135

Hillier, Sir Harold George Knight

Born 2 January 1905, died 8 January 1985
VMH 1957; VMM 1962; knighted 1983;
Lawrence Medal 1960, 1964, 1972, 1982;
Loder Rhododendron Cup 1972;
Rothschild Challenge Cup 1973, 1976

Harold Hillier was the son of Edwin Hillier, who ran a tree and shrub nursery near Winchester. Harold joined in 1921 and became a partner in 1932. The firm had profited from E. H. Wilson's introductions, and was already known for plant breeding – among its creations was x *Halimiocistus wintonensis* (1910), the first bigeneric hybrid of its kind. Harold succeeded his father as Director in 1944, and continued the plant breeding and the foreign introductions. Hilliers went on to receive the longest continuous run of Gold Medals for its displays at the Chelsea Flower Show.

Sir Harold Hillier

In 1952 he bought Jermyns House, near Romsey, and developed its 65-acre site piecemeal over the next 20 years as an arboretum. As he got older, he worried increasingly about the future of his arboretum: 'I was haunted by the thought that some grandchild or great-grandchild might be over tempted to dispose of the site for some form of development.' In 1977 the Harold Hillier Trust was formed, and the Hillier Arboretum formally transferred to Hampshire County Council the following year, to be maintained as a public tree collection.

Apart from his catalogues, Hillier published little; his only book was an Alpine Garden Society pamphlet on *Dwarf Conifers* (1964). But the idea of a comprehensive catalogue of all the trees and shrubs he was growing took hold of him, and with the aid of Roy Lancaster and Hatton Gardener the *Hillier Manual of Trees & Shrubs* was compiled and published in 1971, with 8,000 descriptions in its first edition. **50, 52, 53**

Hodgkin, Eliot

Born 16 December 1905, died 6 March 1973
VMH 1972

Eliot Hodgkin was by profession a commercial traveller for ICI, eventually becoming their Overseas General Manager and retiring in 1968. But he had long since become an eminent horticulturist, travelling with E. B.

Anderson in Europe in search of plants, and serving on the Ministry of Transport's committee on the landscaping of roads. He was President of the Alpine Garden Society from 1971 to 1973, and a Council member of the RHS, as well as a member of six committees, among them the Joint Rock Garden Plant Committee, of which he was for a time Vice-Chairman.

He and his wife Katharine (commemorated in the name of *Iris* 'Katharine Hodgkin') moved to a new garden, Shelleys, near Twyford in Berkshire, in 1950. A 'small garden' by the standards of the period, at 2¼ acres, it was filled by the Hodgkins with irises and other bulbs, dwarf conifers, old-fashioned herbaceous plants, daphnes, variegated plants (especially hollies) and, following the example of E. A. Bowles, a collection of 'lunatics' (varieties of unusual habit). In his last years he became enthusiastic about Japanese irises, making a clearing in the wild part of the garden for them.

Chris Brickell described the garden at Shelleys as 'not merely a repository for a vast collection of plants, but a well-designed and tastefully laid-out garden, colourful throughout the year and fascinating to layman and specialist alike.'

A year before his death he was awarded the VMH, but was too unwell to attend the meeting; Sir Eric Savill and Harold Hillier took the award to him. **99, 102, 103**

Eliot Hodgkin

Ingram, Collingwood

Born 28 October 1880, died 19 May 1981
VMM 1948; VMH, 1952; Reginald Cory
Memorial Cup 1960, 1976; Loder
Rhododendron Cup 1963

Collingwood Ingram earned his nickname of 'Cherry' Ingram through his work introducing Japanese cherry varieties into Europe – among them 'Tai Haku', lost to cultivation in Japan at the time of its rescue – and breeding new cultivars – among them 'Kursar' and 'Okame'. His book *Ornamental Cherries* (1948) remains the most important English monograph on the genus.

But he came late to botany and horticulture, having been an ornithologist first. On acquiring a house and garden in Benenden in Kent in 1919, he made the transition from birds to plants, teaching himself botany from a copy of Lindley's *Introduction to Botany*, a work originally published in 1830. In the interwar years he collected plants together with George Taylor, later the Director of Kew, and Lawrence Johnston of Hidcote. His first article on Japanese cherries appeared in the RHS *Journal* for 1925. Late in life, he was heard to remark that the problem with cherries was that they were so short-lived: 50 years or so and they tended to die.

In addition to cherries, he bred various other shrubs and trees, among them *Rubus* 'Benenden' and *Rhododendron* 'Sarled'. He was twice awarded the Cory Cup for best new hybrid of the year, both times for *Cistus* cultivars: in 1960, for 'Anne Palmer', and in 1976 for 'Blanche'. Anne Palmer had become a friend of his in the 1950s, and they collected plants together in his later years; she built up a collection of his plants at her garden at Rosemoor. He wrote two accounts of his plant collecting: *Isles of the Seven Seas* (1938) and *A Garden of Memories* (1970).

Anne Scott-James described him in the RHS *Journal* in 1975: 'as eager today, at 94, as he was fifty years ago to hybridize rhododendrons, take the wheel of his car,

'Cherry' Ingram

play an advanced game of chess, run up to London for a Flower Show, write a learned monograph, entertain some of his twelve great-grandchildren or take his dog for a walk at 6.30 in the morning.' His centenary was much celebrated in the gardening world: his portrait was on the front cover of *Horticulture Week*. 103, 104, 105, 109

Ingwersen, Will Alfred Theodore

Born 7 May 1905, died 14 June 1990
VMH 1962
Will Ingwersen was the elder son of Walter Ingwersen, the founder of the celebrated Birch Farm Nursery at Gravetye, near East Grinstead. Educated at home, he could remember helping his father at the first Chelsea Flower Show. In 1919, he was apprenticed at the Six Hills Nursery, where his father was working with Clarence Elliott, before going independent in 1925. In 1930 he went to work for Lawrence Johnston at his garden in the south of France, Serre de la Madone. He returned to the family firm, becoming managing director in 1957.

A prolific writer, he produced several books which became classics of the literature on alpine gardening: *The Dianthus* (1949); *Rock Garden Plants* (1965); *Classic Garden Plants* (1975); the Wisley *Handbook on Alpines without a Rock Garden* (1975); and, above all, *Ingwersen's Manual of Alpine Plants* (1978,

1981, 1991). He joined the RHS Floral A Committee in the 1940s, eventually succeeding Geoffrey Pilkington as Chairman, and also spent several years on the Library Committee. He was the only person ever to get away with smoking in the RHS Library, mainly because it seemed impossible to stop him; after committee meetings, the windows of the Librarian's office would be opened for hours, whatever the weather, to dissipate the fumes.

The great project of his later years was the Tehran Botanic Garden, for which in the 1970s he designed a rock garden; but the revolution of 1979 put an end to further development there. 38, 39, 50, 52, 122

Lancaster, Nancy

Born 10 September 1897, died 19 August 1994
Nancy Lancaster, as she was eventually to become, was born Nancy Perkins in Virginia and brought up in America. Her first marriage, to Henry Field, of the Marshall Field department store family, began and ended in 1917, when she was widowed within a few months. She then married a cousin of his, Ronald Field Tree, with whom she moved to England, where he wanted to pursue a political career.

In 1928 they leased Kelmarsh Hall, Northamptonshire, and five years later

bought Ditchley in Oxfordshire; at both estates they hired the young Geoffrey Jellicoe and Russell Page to redesign the gardens. The Trees divorced in 1947, and Nancy married Claude Lancaster, the owner of Kelmarsh Hall, only to go through another divorce in 1951. By this time she had acquired the firm of Colefax and Fowler, and began a new career as Fowler's partner in interior decoration.

In 1954 she acquired Haseley Court in Oxfordshire, where she redesigned the gardens. Russell Page was again called in to assist; an existing topiary garden was refurbished with the aid of her gardener Mr Shepherd; Graham Thomas created a garden of old roses. When Haseley was damaged by fire in 1974, Lancaster sold the house, but retained the walled garden and Coach House, where she lived for the rest of her life. 41, 61, 70–74

MacKenzie, William Gregor

Born 14 January 1904, died 16 October 1995
VMH 1961; AOH 1954; FLS; Lyttel Trophy AGS
Bill MacKenzie was born at Ballimore, in Argyll, where his father was estate manager. He began his gardening apprenticeship there as vegetable boy, responsible for carrying the kitchen garden's produce to the kitchen, and rose to the rank of foreman.

Nancy Lancaster and Haseley Court

In 1928 he began a three-year course at the Edinburgh Botanic Garden, supplemented by additional training at the East of Scotland College. Under Sir William Wright Smith, he became sub-foreman of the seed department at Edinburgh, with special responsibility for primulas, on which Smith was a leading authority. In 1933 he was made assistant curator of the rock garden and herbaceous departments, and laid out the new heather garden. He was also one of the founders of the Scottish Rock Garden Club. His gentian 'Inverleith' was awarded the Reginald Cory Cup by the RHS in 1952; the award was granted to the Botanic Garden, MacKenzie having moved elsewhere.

In January 1946 he took up the post of Curator at the Chelsea Physic Garden; E. A. Bowles had been in charge of the selection panel. Recovery from wartime neglect and damage was the first task: MacKenzie restored the glasshouses, rock garden and the order beds. No longer used by the Society of Apothecaries for teaching purposes, the garden had languished, but was reinvigorated as a horticultural centre during his time. During his vacations he frequently travelled in the Alps, becoming one of the first to conduct alpine plant tours there.

MacKenzie stayed at the Chelsea Physic Garden until its tercentenary in 1973. He was a long-serving member of the Scientific, Orchid, Joint Rock Garden Plant, and Floral B committees of the RHS, and a member of Council. His name is commemorated in *Clematis* 'Bill MacKenzie', propagated and named in 1968 by Valerie Finnis. **25, 42**

McMurtrie, Mary
Born 1902, died 2003
Mary McMurtrie graduated from Gray's School of Art in Aberdeen; her husband John was a parish minister. They grew alpines and florists' flowers at their house

Bill MacKenzie and his wife

at Skene, and after his death in 1949, she moved to Springbank Lodge in Aberdeen, where she ran a nursery in addition to painting. Around 1960 she moved to Balbithan House in Aberdeenshire, where she developed a well-known garden which she opened to the public. It was divided into three sections: a lawn in front of the house, with drifts of naturalized bulbs; the main garden, concealed by a wall, containing a rock garden and rose border; and the commercial nursery.

In the 1970s she began producing illustrated books on plants: *Wild Flowers of the Algarve* (1973), *Wild Flowers of Scotland* (1982), *Scots Roses* (1998), *Scottish Wild Flowers* (2001) and *Old Cottage Pinks* (posthumously, 2004). Shortly before her death she was given an award for being the oldest working artist in Britain. **103, 114, 115**

Mason, Maurice
Born 26 May 1912, died November 1993
VMH 1960; VMM 1968
Maurice Mason was the son of a farmer at Fincham in Norfolk, and after leaving school he joined his father on the farm. In 1932 he bought Talbot Manor, which he increased by later purchases to 40 acres, and here he grew sugar beet and corn; after the War he had a stint of farming on a larger scale in Rhodesia, but returned to Talbot Manor to concentrate

more on the development of its gardens. He became a plant collector on a worldwide scale, travelling to Madagascar, Malaysia, New Guinea, Australia and New Zealand, and South America, usually accompanied by his second wife Margaret. In 1955 *Begonia masoniana*, which he discovered among plants imported from Singapore, won a trophy at the Ghent Floralies.

For nearly 40 years Mason gardened on a massive scale, and kept the Victorian tradition of exotic horticulture alive in his 18 greenhouses, many of them devoted to single categories of plants (bromeliads, begonias, cacti, other succulents, peperomias). He received award after award for his exhibits; in 1980 he filled the monument site at the Chelsea Flower Show with plants from his greenhouses, and received the Lawrence Medal; he won the Williams Memorial Medal three times, for begonias and bromeliads.

But his horticultural activities were not limited to the glasshouse: they ranged from supporting the flower-arranging movement in the 1950s, to amassing a collection of old-fashioned and species roses. He served on the Council of the RHS and on a variety of committees, chairing simultaneously for nearly a decade the Orchid and Floral C Committees, while acting as Vice-Chairman of Floral B.

After the Second World War, Mason had acquired 100 acres of derelict woodland near Talbot Manor, and as aircraft flights over the Manor garden became increasingly intrusive in the 1960s, he built a second house there. Larchwood became an immense woodland garden, second only to Talbot Manor in fame. **82, 85, 87**

Moore, Phylis
Died Dublin 1974
In 1901 Phylis Paul, daughter of the celebrated nurseryman William Paul

(whose name is commemorated in plant names such as 'Paul's Scarlet Climber'), married Sir Frederick Moore (1857–1949), the Director of the National Botanic Garden at Glasnevin, Dublin. After Sir Frederick's retirement in 1922, they moved to Willbrook House outside Dublin, where they created their own 3-acre garden, which became well known among Irish plantsmen for its collections of conifers and magnolias, silver-leaved plants and old roses. They travelled frequently, and in the 1930s helped with the founding of the American Rock Garden Society. After Sir Frederick's death, Lady Moore continued her horticultural activities, and represented the Royal Horticultural Society of Ireland at the RHS Sesquicentennial in 1954.
120, 121

Morris, Sir Cedric Lockwood, 9th Baronet

Born 11 December 1889, died 8 February 1982

Cedric Morris was the son of George Lockwood Morris, later the 8th Baronet, an ironfounder by profession. His health prevented him from joining the army during the First World War, but he joined the Remounts and spent the first years of the War training horses for the front; in 1916 the Army took over the Remounts, and Morris was discharged. He moved to the artists' colony in Newlyn, where he stayed until 1920; it was here he met his life's companion, Arthur Lett-Haines (1894–1978).

During the interwar years Morris was a rising artist; in 1937 he founded the East Anglian School of Painting and Drawing, based first at Dedham and then, from 1940, at his house at Benton End, Hadleigh.

Beth Chatto recalled him as 'elegant in crumpled corduroys, a soft silk scarf around his long neck upon which was a fine head crowned with short-cut waving hair.' At Benton End he increasingly

turned his attention to plant breeding; his pink iris 'Strathmore' was shown at Chelsea in 1948, and the firm of Robert Wallace marketed his introductions in the 1950s. He is also commemorated by the poppy 'Cedric Morris'. His later years saw a revival of interest in his work, and the Tate Gallery has several of his paintings and acquired his papers on his death.
114, 116, 118, 136

Nutbeam, Frederick Charles

Born 18 March 1913, died 16 May 1997
MVO 1977

Fred Nutbeam was born near Fawley in Hampshire, the son of a scaffolder. He had no formal apprenticeship, but effectively trained as a jobbing gardener, eventually working his way up to a post at Walmer Castle in Kent. During the War he served in the Navy as a fire-fighting instructor at Portsmouth, to return to horticulture in 1947 with the post of head gardener at St Donat's Castle.

In 1954 he answered a newspaper advertisement for the post of head gardener at a large private garden in London, and found himself managing the 40-acre gardens of Buckingham Palace for the next quarter of a century. Among his first tasks was the planting of additional trees to help screen the gardens from the increasingly tall buildings of central London. He extended the shrubberies, coped with the great drought of 1976 and fought an annually renewed battle to keep the lawns in good condition despite the erosive effects of visitors at garden parties. In 1972 a gift of silver-leaved plants from Lord and Lady Astor resulted in the creation of a special garden within the garden. Meanwhile he had his own kitchen garden at the Palace.

In 1978 he retired, and moved to Dibden Purlieu in the New Forest, where he made his own garden. He continued his association with the royal gardens, however, and in 1983 he designed the

Princess Alice Memorial Garden in the precincts of Kensington Town Hall.
42, 43

Palmer, Hon. William Jocelyn Lewis

Born 15 September 1894, died 6 June 1971
VMH 1954

Lewis Palmer, known to his friends as 'Luly', was the younger son of the second Earl of Selborne and Lady Maud Cecil. For 20 years he was a member of Hampshire County Council, and was twice Master of the Mercers' Company (1951, 1957). He married Dorothy Loder, the daughter of G. W. E. Loder, later Lord Wakehurst. He was a Council member of the RHS for 30 years; a member, and intermittently Chairman, of its Publications Committee; the Chairman of its Floral B Committee for 12 years; and the Society's Treasurer from 1953 to 1965.

Palmer had five gardens in all: a town garden in London; country gardens successively in Sussex and Hampshire; Headbourne Worthy in Hampshire; and lastly, three years before his death, he began a smaller-scale garden in Guernsey in order to grow dwarf bulbs. This last move was not a success: the sand he used in moving his bulbs had been accidentally impregnated with sodium chlorate and he lost much of his collection. He was a successful plant breeder; his daffodil 'Larkwhistle' received an Award of Merit, and his philadelphus 'Beauclerk' a First Class Certificate. But he was most famous for breeding the Headbourne Hybrid agapanthus, the first important series of hybrids of that genus. He wrote the treatments of *Agapanthus* and *Cyclamen* for the RHS *Dictionary of Gardening* in the 1950s. Sir George Taylor described him as 'the most knowledgeable botanical horticulturist whose friendship I can claim'. In his later years he had a tendency to get people mixed up, and once said that 'If only they were as different as snowdrops, it would be so easy!' 61, 100, 102, 103

Picton, Percy

Born 15 January 1905, died 28 May 1984
AOH 1976

During the 1930s, Percy Picton worked as a gardener for William Robinson on his estate at Gravetye in Sussex. In 1947 he joined the Old Court Nursery at Colwall in Worcestershire, to manage it for the now aging Ernest Ballard, the early 20th century's premier hybridist of Michaelmas daisies. Ballard died in 1951, leaving Picton as Director of the Nursery. Throughout the 1950s and 1960s, Old Court produced a steady stream of aster cultivars. Since Picton's death, his son Paul has continued the nursery, and written *The Gardener's Guide to Growing Asters* (1999).

Percy Picton was president of the Wyche and Colwall Horticultural Society, and a supporter of the nearby Pershore College of Horticulture. After his death, the Percy Picton Memorial Fund was set up by that Society, and continues to provide support for Pershore students. 17, 50, 52

Rothschild, Dame Miriam

Born 5 August 1908, died 20 January 2005
VMH 1990; FRS1985; OBE 2000

Miriam Rothschild was the daughter of Charles Rothschild, banker and naturalist, founder of the Society for the Promotion of Nature Reserves, and an expert on fleas. In that respect she followed in his footsteps, compiling the six-volume *Catalogue of the Rothschild Collection of Fleas*, and going on to study parasitic worms at Plymouth. During the Second World War, when the demand for increased food production was leading to large tracts of land being dug up, she advised on which areas in

Percy Picton

Northamptonshire and Bedfordshire should be retained for nature conservation. She also worked as a codebreaker at Bletchley.

In 1943 she married Captain George Lane, but their marriage was dissolved in 1957. In the 1970s she moved to Ashton Wold, Northamptonshire, where she began to experiment with gardening for conservation purposes. When she arrived, there were 5 acres of formal gardens, and she started by turning nearly an acre of tennis courts into meadows. Her book *The Butterfly Gardener* (1983) was one of the first manuals on gardening for the encouragement of wildlife, and she used her garden to produce a variety of seed mixes, for environments such as waterlogged fields, stream banks and rough grassland, all harvested on a scale which ensured that the mixes preserved the natural proportions of plants. (One of the mixes was endearingly called 'Farmer's Nightmare'.)

She campaigned until the end of her life for organic gardening, and attracted a following that included the Prince of Wales. 74–76

Russell, John Louis

Born 3 March 1897, died 25 February 1976
VMH 1957; Lawrence Medal 1965

John L. Russell was the son of Louis R. Russell (1863–1942), who had founded the Richmond Nurseries, and acquired the businesses of other nurseries in Surrey and Kent. He saw action in the First World War as a gunner, and as a result suffered the rest of his life from deafness. He went to work in the family nursery, and L.R. Russell expected him to set an example by working longer hours than the other staff. In 1924 he was responsible for landscaping the setting of the Australian Pavilion at the British Empire Exhibition at Wembley, thus beginning a long career of designing exhibits for shows, and of landscaping; he was later responsible for planting the beech avenue at Chequers.

In 1936 he moved the firm to Windlesham in Surrey, where it continues to this day, his son Louis having succeeded him; all three Russells have been awarded the Victoria Medal in their turn. He served on the Council of the RHS from 1957 to 1971, and chaired its Shows Committee from 1959 to 1970, as well as playing a role on the Floral B and Rhododendron Committees. 56

Sackville-West, Victoria May

Born 9 March 1892, died 2 June 1962
VMM 1955; CH 1946

Vita Sackville-West was brought up at Knole, in Kent, and moved throughout her life in artistic and literary circles. She wrote novels and poems – including *The Garden* (1946) – as well as travel books and a history of the Women's Land Army. In 1913 she married the writer and diplomat Harold Nicolson. In 1930 they bought Sissinghurst Castle in Kent, and began making a garden there, consisting of a series of hedged enclosures, each with a different theme or horticultural specialty.

Her first gardening book, *Some Flowers*, was published in 1937. In 1947, Sackville-West began a gardening column in the *Observer*, the results of which were collected in a series of books: *In Your Garden* (1951), *In Your Garden Again*

(1953), *More for Your Garden* (1955), and finally *Even More for Your Garden* (1958).

In 1948 she became the first Chairman of the National Trust's joint committee with the RHS on the acquisition of gardens: Hidcote was the first garden thus taken over. The finances of garden acquisition were initially met through another initiative of Sackville-West's: the newly established National Health Service was taking over the Queen's Institute for Nursing, which had been funding itself for 20 years by a programme of garden-opening, and under her direction this programme was reorganized as the National Gardens Scheme. From 1949 to 1955 a percentage of the funds raised was paid to the Joint Committee.

In her later years, Sackville-West hired a pair of Waterperry-trained girls, Pamela Schwerdt and Sibylle Kreutzberger, to assist her in the garden at Sissinghurst. The pair continued to manage the gardens after her death, when Sissinghurst was taken over in its turn by the National Trust. **34, 35, 61, 64, 67–68, 90, 136**

Savill, Sir Eric Humphrey

Born 20 October 1895, died 15 April 1980
VMH 1955; VMM 1963; MVO 1938; CVO 1950, KCVO 1955; CBE 1946; **Loder Rhododendron Cup 1955; Lyttel Lily Cup 1960**
Eric Savill was the son of Sir Edwin Savill, the chartered surveyor and head of the prestigious firm of Savills. During the First World War he served at the Battle of the Somme, winning the Military Cross; he later incurred wounds in the leg and chest. He returned after the War to his interrupted studies at Cambridge, receiving his BA in 1920, and joining his father's firm, of which he became a partner in 1926. He continued his studies on the side, taking his MA in 1930, and in the same year he left Savills to become Deputy Surveyor at Windsor.

As he moved up the hierarchy to become Deputy Ranger (1937), Director of Forestry to the Crown Estate (1958), and Director of Gardens (1959), he devoted much of his time to a special project: the creation of what was to become known as The Savill Garden in Windsor Great Park, a woodland garden in a new style, characterized by glades and vistas, without the emphasis on colour combinations that had characterized the woodland gardens of the previous quarter of a century. (Savill once quipped that it would be better for a gardener to be colour-blind than to get too involved with colour schemes.) The main body of the garden was completed before the Second World War, though it was later to be augmented with a formal garden of herbaceous borders as well as a rose garden.

In 1943 Savill acquired an assistant, (Thomas) Hope Findlay, who assisted him with the later development of the Savill Garden, and with the creation of the great postwar project, the Valley Garden. This included the transplanting of the late John Barr Stevenson's collection of rhododendrons planted in series, from his garden at Tower Court near Ascot.

In 1952 Savill joined the Council of the RHS, on which he served until 1968, eventually becoming a Vice-President, at the same time also serving on the

The Savill Garden

Rhododendron, Publications, and Wisley Advisory Committees. In 1954 he was appointed a member of the Ministry of Transport's committee on the landscaping of roads, which he chaired from 1962 to 1969. He finally retired from Windsor in 1970. **107, 106, 109**

Schacht, Wilhelm

Born 1903, died 2001
Wilhelm Schacht began his horticultural career working for the Royal Parks in Bulgaria. He became a friend of King Boris III, with whom he collected plants in the Alps and the Balkans. He also became a friend of the great German nurseryman Karl Foerster, whose promotion of perennials met with an enthusiastic response from Schacht. He contributed to Max Eiselt's *Freiland-Schmuckstauden* (1950–51), a major monograph on perennials, and took increasing control of the later editions; the third edition (1985) appeared as the joint work of Schacht and Leo Jelitto, and was translated into English in 1990 as *Hardy Herbaceous Perennials.*

The Second World War took its predictable toll of horticultural work, and Schacht left Bulgaria after Boris III's mysterious death in 1943. In 1948 he was appointed Curator of the Munich Botanical Garden at Nymphenburg, where he remained for the next 20 years. Here he developed heather and rhododendron gardens, a spring garden and, on Schachen in the Bavarian Alps, an annexe in the form of an alpine garden.

He became the leading German writer on alpine plants. His *Der Steingarten und seine Welt* (1953) went through several editions, and two different versions of it have been translated into English: by Vera Higgins as *Rock Gardens and their Plants* (1963), and again by Jim Archibald as *Rock Gardens* (1981). **6, 82, 122, 124, 125, 135**

Wilhelm Schacht and his wife

Shackleton, David

Born 1924, died 1988

David Shackleton maintained a fine plant collection in his garden at Beech Park, Clonsilla, near Dublin, where he grew nearly 10,000 species in a 2-acre walled garden. Mollie Sanderson described him as 'its director, clerical staff, collector, curator and gardener, all one man'.

He came under the influence of Valerie Finnis in the early 1960s, when he appeared in a supporting role to her at lectures in Belfast. His collection of some 250 saxifrages was recognized as reflecting her influence. Another special interest was *Celmisia*, about 34 species of which he grew in raised beds, where they were said to grow more vigorously than they did in the wild. He exercised a great influence on a generation of Irish plantsmen. Roy Elliott said, 'I know that a lot of people found him arrogant and rude, but that was just a filter to do away with foolish persons for whom he had little patience.' **56, 57, 118, 120, 121, 122**

Sherriff, George

Born 3 May 1898, died 19 September 1967
VMM 1948; VMH 1953; Loder Rhododendron Cup 1943

George Sherriff, after serving as a gunner in India during the First World War, became Vice-Consul at Kashgar. It was there in 1929 that he met Frank Ludlow, with whom he was to form one of the most important plant-collecting partnerships. Their first expedition was undertaken in 1933, and followed by others in 1934, 1936, 1937, 1938, 1946–47, and 1949 – concentrating on the Himalaya and adjoining areas. In the postwar expeditions, Ludlow and Sherriff pioneered the use of air transport to carry plants back to Europe. Like most of the important 20th-century collectors, they had been financed by syndicates; the RHS had been an important source of funds, and was still trying to persuade them to collect in Nepal when they retired.

Rhododendrons were the great selling point of their expeditions, and the RHS at one point planned a book of their rhododendron introductions. Sherriff, however, was also interested in alpine plants, and one of his most famous discoveries was *Primula sherriffae*, which has now disappeared from commerce. At his garden at Ascreavie in Scotland, Sherriff created a garden modelled on the Himalayan vegetation with which he was familiar, and developed it with his wife Betty, who had taken part in the team's later expeditions. Harold Fletcher's account of their journeys, *A Quest of Flowers*, was published in 1975.
109, 110, 111, 112

Stearn, William Thomas

Born 16 April 1911, died 9 May 2001
VMH 1965; VMM 1964; Lyttel Lily Cup 1986

Sometimes referred to as 'the modern Linnaeus', W. T. Stearn never had a formal university education. He was working as an assistant in Bowes and Bowes' bookshop in Cambridge when he was discovered by E. A. Bowles, and invited to become the Librarian of the Royal Horticultural Society. He had already published his first botanical paper, had spent his spare time studying at the Cambridge Botanic Garden and was working on a monograph on *Epimedium* – the subject of his first taxonomic revision, published in the Linnean Society's *Journal* in 1934. He returned to it in later years, *The Genus Epimedium* appearing posthumously in 2002.

Apart from wartime service, Stearn worked in the RHS Lindley Library from 1932 until the end of 1951, when he moved to the Botany Library of the Natural History Museum. During his 20 years with the RHS, he was responsible for representing the Society at the International Botanical Congress in Stockholm in 1950, drafting the first version of the International Code of Nomenclature for Cultivated Plants; and helped to complete the RHS *Dictionary of Gardening* after the death of the original compiler, Frederick Chittenden – in the process becoming, in his own words, an expert on plants from 'So to Z'.

Three of Stearn's many works have become indispensable: *Botanical Latin* (1966 and later editions), his revision of A. W. Smith's *Gardener's Dictionary of Plant Names* (1971 and later editions), and his collaboration with Wilfrid Blunt on *The Art of Botanical Illustration* (1950; rev. 1994). But the list also includes monographs such as *Peonies of Greece*, histories of botany such as the introduction to the facsimile reprint of Linnaeus's *Species Plantarum*, and his history of *The Natural History Museum at South Kensington*. **114**

J. M. Brenan and W. T. Stearn

An Alpine Garden Society plant sale, Kent

Stern, Sir Frederick Claude

Born 8 April 1884, died 10 July 1967
VMH 1940; knighted 1956; VMM 1960;
Engleheart Cup 1944; Lyttel Lily Cup 1942,
1961; Peter Barr Memorial Cup 1952
Sir Frederick Stern was a merchant banker
by profession, and in his time held such
other positions as Assistant Private
Secretary to Lloyd George, and Master
of the Drapers' Company. His first
important leisure activity was big game
hunting, but by the First World War he
had turned in the direction of
horticulture. In 1914 he was one of the
subscribers to Reginald Farrer's
Himalayan expedition, and received
various species of lilies and gentians, and
Viburnum farreri. Five years earlier he had
acquired his garden at Highdown, near
Worthing in Sussex, a disused quarry site,
which he was to develop into the most
famous example in Britain of gardening
on chalk. Already by 1925 his collections
were so extensive that a list was published
in the *Kew Bulletin* under the title 'Flora
Highdownensis'.

He first joined an RHS committee in
1922, and eventually served on Council
from 1931 to 1964. He was one of the
instigators of the RHS Lily Group, and
helped to get Grove and Cotton's
Supplement to Elwes's *Monograph of the
Genus Lilium* published; he was twice to
be awarded the Lyttel Cup for his work
with lilies. He also received awards for
daffodils, and twice received the Cory

Cup for the best new hybrid of the year,
once for *Rosa* 'Highdownensis' and once
for *Paeonia* 'Emma'. His plant breeding
was extensive and varied, encompassing
new cultivars of snowdrops, thymes,
euonymus, irises, helianthemums, peonies
and the Highdown Hybrid series of
Eremurus, an enthusiasm of his later years.

He published two plant monographs
for the RHS: *A Study of the Genus Paeonia*
in 1946, and *Snowdrops and Snowflakes* in
1956, the latter incorporating the material
E. A. Bowles had been collecting towards
a monograph on the subject. In 1960 he
published an account of the development
of Highdown, *A Chalk Garden*. After his
death, Highdown was taken over by
Worthing Borough Council, who have
maintained it and kept it open.   **56, 57**

Synge, Patrick Millington

Born 17 September 1910, died 16 August
1982
VMM 1957; VMH 1969; Lyttel Lily Cup 1965
Patrick Synge began his horticultural
career as a plant hunter. He took part in
an expedition to Sarawak in 1932, and
then to East Africa, a journey which he
described in his first book, *Mountains of
the Moon* (1938). A quarter of a century
was to pass before his next expedition. In
1937 he became director of the publishing
house of Lindsay Drummond. In 1946 he
was appointed Editor of the *Journal of the
Royal Horticultural Society*, a post he held
until 1969, bringing colour photographs
into the *Journal* for the first time. In 1960
he was granted time off for another plant
collecting expedition – to Turkey and
western Asia with Paul Furse; and further
travels followed in his later years, along
with the editorship of the International
Dendrology Society's *Yearbook*.

Among his books are: *Plants with
Personality* (1939); *Flowers in Winter*
(1948); *A Diversity of Plants* (1953); the
Collins Guide to Bulbs (1961); the RHS
Dictionary of Garden Plants in Colour,

Patrick Synge

with Roy Hay (1969); *In Search of Flowers*
(1973), an account of his later travels. But
his intended *magnum opus* was a revision
of Elwes's *Monograph of the Genus Lilium*.
He worked on this throughout the 1960s
and 1970s; Margaret Stones made new
drawings for it; but conflict with John
Hamer, the Secretary of the RHS, led to
frustrations and delays, and a dispute over
the ownership of the drawings. *Lilies* was
finally published in 1980, and remains the
standard revision of the genus.   **109, 112**

Talbot de Malahide, Milo John Reginald Talbot, 7th Baron

Born 1 December 1912, died at sea 14 April
1973
Described as the most knowledgeable Irish
gardener of his time, Lord Talbot de
Malahide inherited Malahide Castle, near
Dublin, in 1948. His diplomatic career
took him to Vietnam and Laos, and after
his retirement he travelled extensively in
Australia, Afghanistan, South America and
Africa, collecting plants. Australia was
particularly important to him, and he
financed the publication of one of the
20th-century's major floras, *The Endemic
Flora of Tasmania* by Winifred Curtis and
Margaret Stones. He built up an impressive
collection of southern-hemisphere plants
at Malahide Castle, and experimented in
their cultivation. When the known stock
of a wild plant was destroyed by bush fire
in Tasmania, he was able to supply plants

from his own collection to re-establish it in its native lands.

Through correspondence and seed exchange, Lord Talbot maintained what has been described as the largest private botanical network of his time, receiving plants from collectors such as David Shackleton and Martyn Rix. His work was cut short in 1973, when he died without a direct heir. Dublin County Council purchased Malahide Castle in 1976, and preserved his garden: one of the largest purchases made by a local authority in Ireland up to that point. 118, 120, 121, 123

Taylor, Sir George

Born 15 February 1904, died 13 November 1993
VMH 1955; VMM Silver 1934, Gold 1963; knighted 1962; FRS 1968; Scottish Horticultural Medal 1984

George Taylor received a first in Botany from Edinburgh University, and put his skills to work in an expedition to South Africa and Zimbabwe. Africa continued to be important in his career; in 1934, after having worked for the British Museum (Natural History) for six years, he mounted an expedition to Ruwenzori, described by his companion Patrick Synge in *Mountains of the Moon* (1938). But he also travelled to Bhutan with Ludlow and Sherriff in 1938, partly in

Lord Talbot de Malahide and David Shackleton

search of meconopsis, the subject of his only full-length book, *An Account of the Genus Meconopsis* (1934).

After a stint with the Air Ministry during the War, he returned to the Natural History Museum, becoming Keeper of Botany in 1950. In 1951 he joined the Council of the RHS for a long and active association. In 1956 he was appointed Director of the Royal Botanic Gardens, Kew – at the time suffering from post-war depression, underfunding and with buildings in need of such repair that the demolition of the Palm House was being seriously discussed. Taylor, as skilled in fundraising as in botany and horticulture, arranged its (first) restoration, commissioned a new building for the Jodrell Laboratory and a new library and herbarium complex on the other side of Kew Green, initiated several relandscaping projects, and in 1969 oversaw the creation of the Queen's Garden. He retired in 1971, full of honours, and entered into new duties as Chairman of the Chelsea Physic Garden's management committee and Director of the Stanley Smith Horticultural Trust (1970–89). He also served on the Ministry of Transport's advisory committee on the landscaping of roads, which he chaired from 1969 to 1981. He was married four times, and enjoyed acting the role of the blunt and dour Scotsman.   103

Thomas, Graham Stuart

Born 3 April 1909, died 17 April 2003
VMH 1968; VMM 1966

Graham Stuart Thomas joined the staff of the Cambridge Botanic Garden aged 17, before becoming a nurseryman, the role in which he was known during the first half of his career. He began by working for Clarence Elliott at the Six Hills Nursery in 1930, and the following year moved to T. Hilling & Co, of which he later became a director. He was much influenced by Gertrude Jekyll, of whom

David Scott and George Taylor (right)

he became a friend during her last years. It was while working for Hilling that he wrote his first pamphlets on roses and perennials. In 1956, with James Russell, he joined the long-established firm of Sunningdale, near Woking, where he attempted to build up a collection of all the rose cultivars that had been grown in England. The Sunningdale rose collection became famous, but most of it was ploughed under in the 1970s when the firm was absorbed by Waterers. But Thomas had long since become England's leading authority on the history of roses, and his trilogy on the subject – especially *The Old Shrub Roses* (1955) and *Climbing Roses Old and New* (1965) – went on being reprinted for a generation.

By the time he joined Sunningdale, Thomas had already entered the second phase of his career. In 1948 the National Trust embarked on a programme of acquiring important gardens, initially under the auspices of a joint committee established with the RHS. Hidcote was the first acquisition, and Thomas began to assist with the garden almost immediately. In 1955 he was officially appointed the first Gardens Adviser to the Trust, a post he held until retirement in 1974, though continuing as a consultant long after. In this way he became responsible for an increasing number of historic gardens around the country, which he described self-effacingly in his *Gardens of the National Trust* (1979). He

Mrs Joe Elliott, with son Martin

was thus able in effect to establish a collective museum of the history of gardening; he was a founder member and keen supporter of the Garden History Society. His own favourite of the Trust's gardens was Mottisfont Abbey, where he was able to design a rose garden to his own exacting specifications.

Retirement set him free to write on a larger scale than before. In addition to the rose trilogy, he had already written *Colour in the Winter Garden* (1957) and *Plants for Ground Cover* (1970). He now revised and expanded one of his Sunningdale pamphlets into *Perennial Garden Plants: The Modern Florilegium* (1976), which became the major manual on its subject; eventually it had a companion volume on *Ornamental Shrubs, Climbers and Bamboos* (1992). In addition, he wrote a dozen other books, including his autobiography, *Three Gardens* (1983). A long-standing RHS committee member (Floral B, Joint Rock Garden, Library), he was a familiar figure at the London shows into his 90s, always sporting a buttonhole chosen to challenge his fellow horticulturists' abilities at plant identification. 47, 68, 73, 120

Thrower, Percy John
Born 30 January 1913, died 18 March 1988
VMH 1973; AOH 1962

Percy Thrower was a gardener's son, and by the age of 14 he was working for his

father in the garden of Horwood House. At 18, he moved to the Royal Garden at Windsor, then under the direction of C. H. Cook, whose daughter Constance he later married. He next entered the municipal parks service, working first at Leeds and then at Derby, where he was active in the Dig for Victory campaign during the War.

In 1946 he became Superintendent of Parks at Shrewsbury, where he spent most of his career. He revived the Shrewsbury Flower Show, making it one of the country's leading shows. He also began a career as a broadcaster, first on the radio in 1946, and then television in 1952, commenting on gardening matters successively on Picture Page, Country Calendar, Gardening Club, and finally, in 1969, Gardeners' World. His own garden at The Magnolias, the house he bought in 1963, became the first Gardeners' World demonstration site. His association with that programme was cut short in 1976, when he appeared in advertisements on ITV, and the resolutely non-commercial BBC terminated his contract.

When Thrower retired he took over the late Edwin Murrell's long-established rose nursery in Shrewsbury. He had already published many books, beginning with *In the Flower Garden with Percy Thrower* (1957); his autobiography, *My Lifetime of Gardening,* appeared in 1977. Often described as Britain's most popular

The Plantsmen: Jim Archibald and Eric Smith

gardener, he was treated with disdain for much of his career by part of the gardening establishment for his association with television. 17, 42, 44, 45

Trotter, Richard Durant
Born 1887, died 20 March 1968
VMH 1952

Dick Trotter was a banker by profession, a Director of the National Provincial Bank, and later Chairman of the Alliance Assurance Company. He joined the Council of the Royal Horticultural Society in 1928, and served as its Treasurer in 1929–32, 1933–38 and 1943–48. He was also a member of the Royal Company of Archers.

During the 1920s he travelled with E. A. Bowles to the Alps and Greece, collecting plants. He had three gardens in succession, beginning with his family home, The Bush, Midlothian. Leith Vale, in Surrey, was his home with his wife from the late 1920s, and his sole garden from the Second World War, when the army took over The Bush.

Some years after the War he sold Leith Vale and retired to Brin House, near Inverness. The soil here was too acid even for his rhododendrons, so he concentrated on herbaceous plants. He raised eponymous forms of snowdrops, hellebores, tulips, colchicums and *Caltha palustris*. 94, 108

Wada, Koichiro
Dates of birth and death not ascertained

Wada's Hakoneya Nurseries, in Numazu-shi in Japan, came to international prominence in the 1930s. Wada announced a new method of packing bulbs for export, using a mixture of quasi-volcanic grainy earth and sawdust. which ensured a higher survival rate than ordinary packing. By the end of the decade he was offering specialist catalogues for lilies, irises, peonies,

A Japanese garden and Koichiro Wada

cherries, camellias, azaleas, primulas and alpines. He bred or selected many cultivars, some of which, like *Saxifraga* 'Wada' and *Magnolia salicifolia* 'Wada's Memory' (named by Brian Mulligan in the 1940s, while Wada was very much alive and active), became popular in the West – not to mention Japanese maples, from 'Butterfly' in the 1930s to 'Tsuma Beni' in the 1960s. It was Wada who, by sending two specimens of *Rhododendron yakushimanum* to Exbury in the 1930s, sparked the fashion for this species; and the Kurume azaleas he supplied to John Barr Stevenson at Tower Court were later transplanted to the Valley Garden in Windsor Great Park to form the basis of the famous Kurume Punch Bowl. **18, 109**

Warburg, Primrose

Born 23 November 1891, died 24 November 1996

Primrose Churchman was associated with the Oxford Botanic Garden, and an expert in petaloid monocots such as snowdrops, when she met Edmund Frederick Warburg (1908–66). Warburg was the curator of the Druce Herbarium at Oxford, President of the Botanical Society of the British Isles and editor of its journal *Watsonia*, and co-author of Clapham, Tutin and Warburg's *Flora of the British Isles*. They married in 1948.

The couple lived at Yarnells Hill, Oxford, where they grew crocuses and other hardy plants. Primrose became famous for her collections of old roses, willows and curious vegetable cultivars, and after Edmund's death she continued to be active as a raiser of bulbs. Shortly after she died, in February 1997, a group of snowdrop enthusiasts met to honour and discuss her legacy. One result of the meeting was that a new cultivar with a yellow ovary was named 'Primrose Warburg' in her honour. **98, 99, 100**

Warre, Norah Mosson

Born 5 March 1880, died 3 July 1979

Norah Warre's first husband was Emerson Bainbridge, who bought the Villa Roquebrune near Menton in 1902. On being shown the steep, arid site, Norah is said to have burst into tears and said, 'But I wanted to make a garden'. Work began on terracing the site. After Bainbridge's death, Norah married George Warre, and work on the 5-acre site continued, with help from her neighbour Lawrence Johnston (who was making his Mediterranean garden Serre de la Madone at the same time), and plants from Kew, Wisley and eventually Hilliers. The original planting of olive trees and conifers was supplemented by a wide range of trees and shrubs, agaves, climbing plants, and bulbs.

Patrick Synge published an account of the garden in the RHS *Journal* in 1966, helping to bring it to wider attention.

The news of Mrs Warre's death was greeted with despondency: 'The garden is unlikely to survive her', wrote Hugh Johnson in *The Garden*. **82, 124**

Wyatt, Oliver E. P.

Born 7 March 1898, died 25 February 1973
VMH 1965

Oliver Wyatt served as Treasurer of the Royal Horticultural Society from 1965 to 1971. His tenure of this office saw the introduction of VAT; Wyatt's efforts to rescue the Society from disaster resulted in the discontinuation of its celebrated *Year Books*, and the creation of its commercial arm, RHS Enterprises.

Before this, Wyatt had been a schoolteacher. He bought Maidwell Hall, Northamptonshire, in 1933 from Robert Loder's family; he ran it as a private school and the Oliver Wyatt Foundation continues to fund it. Wyatt was a bulb enthusiast, with an immense expertise in winter-flowering bulbs; but his greatest love was lilies. He got his first lily seeds (*Cardiocrinum giganteum*) from E. G. Millais, and went on to contribute many rare lilies to the *Supplement* to Elwes's *Monograph of the Genus Lilium*. He raised the parryi hybrids, and made the first cross between a European and an American lily; he named it 'Kelmarsh', but later said 'Perhaps it should have been called "Sir Winston"!' **99**

Norah Warre and Constance Finnis

Picking apples *Vegetable garden with greenhouse* *Winter: Boughton House lake*

ACKNOWLEDGMENTS

There are a number of people whose help in the preparation of this book has been invaluable, help which it gives me great pleasure to acknowledge here. First and foremost, I owe a huge debt to Howard Sooley, whose admiration for Valerie and her photographs led him to approach Thames & Hudson, with a view to publication, and who patiently reviewed the enormous archive of transparencies with Valerie, so that they could pick out the best and most suitable. Without his enthusiasm and encouragement, I doubt whether this book could have come to fruition. I thank him also for permission to use his photograph of Valerie on page 134.

I am also enormously grateful to Dr Brent Elliott, Librarian and Archivist at the Royal Horticultural Society, for providing such scholarly and complete biographies of the photographic subjects, which I trust will enable the reader to build up a fascinating picture of post-war horticulture in Britain and Ireland. His advice, freely and frequently given, as well as his meticulous approach to garden history, have made my task so much easier and more enjoyable.

Great thanks also to Anna Pavord who kindly agreed to allow her obituary of Valerie to appear in the book, reprinted by permission from *The Independent*, Obituaries, 21 October 2006.

I also acknowledge an important debt to Nigel Colborn, for allowing me to draw freely on his article on Valerie, 'Cushion Saxifrages and Cameras', published in 1988 in *Hortus*. This formed the basis of the biographical details about her. Also most useful was *Waterperry – A Dream Fulfilled* (1990) by Ursula Maddy, without which it would have been impossible to give an informed account of that extraordinary establishment.

Chris Brickell, David Curtis, Jane Curtis, Brian Mathew, Bill Meredith, Paul Picton and Charles Shackleton all answered importunate questions and were most helpful. Dr Charles Nelson deserves a medal for the time and trouble he took trying to track down the details of one unknown gardener. I thank them all most sincerely. I am also very grateful to the Earl and Countess of Dalkeith for their encouragement and support of this project.

Lastly, I should like to thank the team at Thames & Hudson. It has been a pleasure to collaborate with them.

This book perforce contains only a small selection of the many portraits which Valerie took. As it is also a chronicle of her life, the tendency has been to choose those people whom she met during her gardening heyday. It is a pity, but inevitable, that many other fine gardeners and friends cannot be included.

Valerie at an exhibition of her pictures *David Scott, with pug* *Memorial to David Scott*